THE GREENHAVEN PRESS COMPANION TO
Literary Movements and Genres

Victorian Literature

Clarice Swisher, *Book Editor*

David L. Bender, *Publisher*

Bruno Leone, *Executive Editor*

Bonnie Szumski, *Editorial Director*

David M. Haugen, *Managing Editor*

Greenhaven Press, Inc., San Diego, CA

Every effort has been made to trace the owners of copyrighted material. The articles in this volume may have been edited for content, length, and/or reading level. The titles have been changed to enhance the editorial purpose. Those interested in locating the original source will find the complete citation on the first page of each article.

Library of Congress Cataloging-in-Publication Data

Victorian literature / Clarice Swisher, book editor.
    p.   cm. — (Literary movements and genres)
    Includes bibliographical references and index.
    ISBN 0-7377-0209-5 (lib. bdg. : alk. paper). —
ISBN 0-7377-0208-7 (pbk. : alk. paper)
    1. English literature—19th century—History and criticism. 2. Great Britain—History—Victoria, 1837–1901. I. Swisher, Clarice, 1933– . II. Series.
PR463.V528   2000
820.9'008—dc21   99-38376
                                                      CIP

Cover photo: Planet Art

Editor's Note: The article on page 152 entitled "The Epic Heritage of *Wuthering Heights*," previously appeared in *Readings on* Wuthering Heights, edited by Hayley R. Mitchell. The article on page 161 previously appeared in *Readings on* Jane Eyre, edited by Jill Karson.

Copyright ©2000 by Greenhaven Press, Inc.
PO Box 289009
San Diego, CA 92198-9009
Printed in the U.S.A.

CONTENTS

Chapter 1: The Era of Reform

When the authority of the church and the aristocracy
broke down in the early 1800s, writers filled the void.
Essayists publishing in periodicals gave intellectual and
moral guidance, and poets and novelists offered inspiration, support, and escape.

Although advised by influential Romantic poet Percy
Bysshe Shelley to ignore tradition when striving for social
change, many Victorian writers rejected his advice as impractical and chose to stay with traditional institutions.
Only toward the end of the Victorian era did writers embrace Shelley's agenda to look beyond traditional authority
in seeking social progress.

Many Victorian prose writers criticized the industrial, materialistic age with great intensity, attacking its effect on
the poor, on the individual, and on public taste.

Chapter 2: The Character of Victorian Writing

In a time of many great social changes, writers regarded
their mission as social commentators with great earnestness and spoke to their readers in an accessible yet imperative tone. Most authors rejected aloof and ornate language and addressed readers in didactic prose.

it. Three poets—Tennyson, Browning, and Arnold—accommodated readers by creating new techniques allowing them to express their private insights in subtle ways.

Tennyson excelled in creating beautiful lyrical poetry. The lines of his verses create the right meter and rhythm and the right combinations of vowel and consonant sounds to make beautiful sound. Even when the content of Tennyson's poems lacks substance, the poetry is good.

Browning's dramatic monologues each have an illuminating moment, a focal point evoking heightened insight, awareness, or experience so intense that time and space seem to compress into that single human moment. These epiphanies may be emotional, aesthetic, or religious.

Matthew Arnold's version of the Victorian search for knowledge and truth portrays narrators trying to find a balance point between active involvement in the world and withdrawal from it. Unable to find and sustain such a place, some of his characters give up and others withdraw further and die.

Chapter 4: The Novelists

Of the major novelists of the period, Dickens—his characters, his storytelling, and his humor—is the star who depicts the lower classes. Thackeray and Trollope portray the daily lives of the higher classes with a quiet realism. The Brontës, Charlotte and Emily, introduced passion and emotional intensity into the Victorian novel.

The male protagonists in Victorian novels are not romantic heroes in the usual sense; they are preferably rich genteel men without vanity and pride. They possess a respect for tradition, but they also respond compassionately to social ills paralleled in the Victorian world.

Wuthering Heights makes powerful use of its storytelling narrator and character monologues. Brontë draws heavily on traditions of oral narratives and epic poetry, such as ballads, throughout the novel.

FOREWORD

The study of literature most often involves focusing on an individual work and uncovering its themes, stylistic conventions, and historical relevance. It is also enlightening to examine multiple works by a single author, identifying similarities and differences among texts and tracing the author's development as an artist.

While the study of individual works and authors is instructive, however, examining groups of authors who shared certain cultural or historical experiences adds a further richness to the study of literature. By focusing on literary movements and genres, readers gain a greater appreciation of influence of historical events and social circumstances on the development of particular literary forms and themes. For example, in the early twentieth century, rapid technological and industrial advances, mass urban migration, World War I, and other events contributed to the emergence of a movement known as American modernism. The dramatic social changes, and the uncertainty they created, were reflected in an increased use of free verse in poetry, the stream-of-consciousness technique in fiction, and a general sense of historical discontinuity and crisis of faith in most of the literature of the era. By focusing on these commonalities, readers attain a more comprehensive picture of the complex interplay of social, economic, political, aesthetic, and philosophical forces and ideas that create the tenor of any era. In the nineteenth-century American romanticism movement, for example, authors shared many ideas concerning the preeminence of the self-reliant individual, the infusion of nature with spiritual significance, and the potential of persons to achieve transcendence via communion with nature. However, despite their commonalities, American romantics often differed significantly in their thematic and stylistic approaches. Walt Whitman celebrated the communal nature of America's open democratic society, while Ralph Waldo

Emerson expressed the need for individuals to pursue their own fulfillment regardless of their fellow citizens. Herman Melville wrote novels in a largely naturalistic style whereas Nathaniel Hawthorne's novels were gothic and allegorical.

Another valuable reason to investigate literary movements and genres lies in their potential to clarify the process of literary evolution. By examining groups of authors, literary trends across time become evident. The reader learns, for instance, how English romanticism was transformed as it crossed the Atlantic to America. The poetry of Lord Byron, William Wordsworth, and John Keats celebrated the restorative potential of rural scenes. The American romantics, writing later in the century, shared their English counterparts' faith in nature; but American authors were more likely to present an ambiguous view of nature as a source of liberation as well as the dwelling place of personal demons. The whale in Melville's *Moby-Dick* and the forests in Hawthorne's novels and stories bear little resemblance to the benign pastoral scenes in Wordsworth's lyric poems.

Each volume in Greenhaven Press's Great Literary Movements and Genres series begins with an introductory essay that places the topic in a historical and literary context. The essays that follow are carefully chosen and edited for ease of comprehension. These essays are arranged into clearly defined chapters that are outlined in a concise annotated table of contents. Finally, a thorough chronology maps out crucial literary milestones of the movement or genre as well as significant social and historical events. Readers will benefit from the structure and coherence that these features lend to material that is often challenging. With Greenhaven's Great Literary Movements and Genres in hand, readers will be better able to comprehend and appreciate the major literary works and their impact on society.

INTRODUCTION

Victorian literature comprises works written during the almost seventy years that Queen Victoria ruled England (1837–1901). Under Victoria, English society changed rapidly and dramatically, and Victorian literature is closely linked to the history of the period. During this time, England became the first Western nation to industrialize and to accomplish this feat peacefully. A factory system developed to manufacture goods. The middle class prospered as never before and wielded new political power. Workers, who flocked to factory cities faster than the cities could accommodate them, suffered from poverty and harsh living and working conditions. After a long struggle, they too gained political influence and a better standard of living. As if these social changes were not sufficiently destabilizing, the Victorian age was also a period of scientific discovery that challenged traditional religious beliefs. Faith in God did not diminish, but faith in technology and scientifically discerned facts expanded. Moreover, during this period large numbers of citizens learned to read and were eager to acquire facts and information as well as enjoy entertainment from the printed word.

These major changes occurred in a relatively short period of time, and Victorian writers responded to them in a variety of ways. Some writers impartially documented the changes; others offered opinions, mostly condemning materialism, the pursuit of money, and the coarsening of culture. A few of the latter became passionate reformers who tried to incite readers to take action against the injustices and ugliness brought about by a society in transition. Poets, on the other hand, tried to stay out of the confusion, idealizing the past and burying themselves in nature and the concerns of art. But even they were not immune to the changes going on around them.

A study of Victorian literature therefore provides a glimpse of English society as it moved into the industrial age. The entire process and its inherent changes in gender roles, class structure, and social values were documented in the pages of Victorian novels, essays, and poems. And even as the nation was coming of age, so were the literary forms in use. Victorian novelists were developing story-telling techniques, deriving the first psychological novels, and experimenting with ways to use symbols in long stories. Speaking of the rise of the English novel, Lionel Stevenson, one of the contributors in this volume, says, "In fact, one of the most compelling reasons for studying Victorian fiction is that it offers a unique opportunity for observing a new literary genre in the very process of maturing." Victorian poets, struggling with the decision of whether to teach moral lessons or to create art, were also paving the way for their literary progeny. The poets' mastery of imagery, symbol, and musical rhythms influenced the shape of poetry to come.

Finally, to study Victorian literature is to find interesting and enjoyable reading. Nonfiction prose offers scientific and religious arguments, political and economic ideas, and ethical and moral advice. Poetry offers beautiful imagery, challenging interpretation, and rhythms to please the ear. Victorian novels offer a multitude of intriguing characters and heartfelt stories. It is these aspects of Victorian literature—whether an infamous character or a particularly memorable line of poetry—that have transcended their own period or genre and continue to echo through literary history and contemporary culture.

Victorian Literature: An Overview

Literary critics generally agree that Victorian literature comprises works written between 1830 and 1900, the period named for Queen Victoria, who reigned as queen of England from 1837 to 1901. Although the queen herself influenced the literature of the age to a small degree, events in English society had far greater significance. The Victorian period was a time of great changes that disrupted economic, social, political, and intellectual traditions. England was entering the industrial age; its agricultural way of life was supplanted by an urban society dependent on the manufacture of goods in factories. Moreover, it was a time of technological and scientific discovery, and newfound faith in scientific research and technological advances challenged traditional religious belief. Citizens in all walks of life were aware of the rapid changes going on around them; Victorian writers produced works in a variety of styles as they reflected on and responded to these changes.

The Industrial Age

The Industrial Revolution had already turned England into an industrialized nation by the time Victoria took the throne. The invention of the coal-powered steam engine in the late eighteenth century gave rise to factories that produced everything from textiles to iron, and the network of railroads rapidly built to connect all parts of the island allowed factory owners to transport raw materials to their factories and manufactured goods to markets. Because steam engines burned coal, the mining industry also grew rapidly to keep up with the increasing demand for coal.

The need for workers to operate the factories drew thousands from rural areas to industrial cities. There, men, women, and children toiled long hours for low wages, returning from work each night to the slums that arose throughout factory towns. The plight of the poor became a concern for many social critics who noticed the widening gap between the haves and the have-nots. Critic John Morley commented that England was becoming "a paradise for the well-to-do, a purgatory for the able, and a hell for the poor."[1] The industrialization of Britain had impoverished many, but it had also brought newfound prosperity to the entrepreneurial middle class. This merchant class, which lacked the hereditary entitlement to wealth afforded the aristocracy, became in the eyes of many writers the oppressors of the poor and the undeserving rivals of the nobility.

THE RISE OF THE MIDDLE CLASS

The fortunes of the middle class defined the economic shifts in Victorian England. Middle-class entrepreneurs started small factories and then funneled profits into increasing expansion. This growth was accompanied by a rise in banking, marketing, and trade, all run by middle-class managers. By the mid–nineteenth century the middle class held a vast share of the nation's wealth. At the same time the upper classes had lost a large part of their wealth because most of the landed gentry owned large estates geared toward agriculture, which was a declining industry.

The rise of the middle class coincided with the advent of philosophical concepts that seemed to lend credence to the ethics of industrialization. Philosopher and reformer Jeremy Bentham promoted utilitarianism, which propounded that what is most useful is most good, and that the aim of action should be to bring the greatest happiness to the greatest number of people. If material wealth made people happy (because money brought a higher standard of living, improved health care, and access to better education), then individuals should be allowed to compete and pursue that good without hindrance. This philosophy supported the economic theory of laissez-faire, the belief that a market economy will regulate itself without governmental interference. These ideas led to the concept of the rugged individual, who was tough enough to compete and succeed, and the middle-class work ethic, which glorified hard work as a means to rise socially and economically.

The newly prosperous middle class was eager to display its wealth and soon dominated social mores and standards of taste. Middle-class Victorians valued whatever was decorative. They built large, ornate homes; they furnished rooms with heavy carved furniture and elaborately designed wallpaper, and filled spaces with decorative knickknacks and bric-a-brac. Men dressed in suits and top hats, and women dressed in long, full-skirted dresses designed with ruffles, bows, and braids. They promenaded on fashionable streets and showed themselves in carriage rides through popular gathering places such as London's Hyde Park.

THE MORAL AND POLITICAL CLIMATE OF VICTORIAN ENGLAND

Having inherited moral values from the Puritans, the middle class preached and supposedly followed a strict moral code. At its core was the notion that the home is an honorable and sacred place. It was Queen Victoria herself who led the effort to make domestic purity fashionable. References to sex were taboo, and scandal, real or rumored, meant social rejection. Because pleasure and entertainment were considered wicked, the moral code prohibited dancing, card playing, and attending the theater. Middle-class morality was also tied to material prosperity. For men, personal qualities that showed a strong work ethic and self-discipline were admired. A proper middle-class woman, on the other hand, was idle, a sign that her prosperous husband could afford the servants to free her from work. All persons were to exhibit qualities such as integrity, frugality, self-reliance, and temperance. Historian Anthony Wood notes, "There is an almost suffocating sobriety about English social life in the mid-Victorian period that has an atmosphere entirely its own."[2] Victorians were intolerant of others' lapses in conduct, but few could live up to such strict expectations themselves. Therefore, Victorians gained a reputation for hypocrisy.

In the political arena, middle-class Victorians were eager to use their economic status to gain a foothold in national policy making. At the beginning of the Industrial Revolution, only the upper class had voting rights and representation in Parliament. By the early 1830s, however, mounting pressure from the poor and middle classes—which often turned violent—persuaded Parliament to extend the franchise. The First Reform Bill, passed in 1832, gave the middle class some representation in Parliament and granted one hundred thousand middle-class men the right to vote. Because the middle class profited from a large pool of poor and powerless workers, the middle class joined the upper classes in limiting further political reform despite a movement in the late 1830s demanding universal suffrage. Eventually, in part because of writers who raised their voices against the injustices perpetrated against the lower classes, enfranchisement was further expanded. The Second Reform Bill, passed in 1867, gave voting rights to lower-class male workers in cities, and the Third Reform Bill of 1884 finally granted voting rights to male agricultural workers. Women, whose attention was supposed to be directed in the home, were still banned from participating in politics.

THE WRITERS RESPOND

Many Victorian nonfiction writers began their careers writing history, biography, and essays on a variety of experiences and ideas, but gradually felt it their duty to comment on the changes surrounding them and addressed social issues. Angered by the negative aspects of rapid industrialization, they collectively denounced "this reliance on machinery and insisted that spiritual regeneration was the only way of social salvation."[3] They directed their wrath at the middle-class Liberal Party, promoters of laissez-faire economics. In their writings, these authors used the machine as both the cause and symbol for the declining emotional vitality of their age. The machine symbolized "progress," and its rhythms had a destructive effect on psychic life by dulling the senses and making people soft and unnatural. In "Signs of the Times," published in 1829, Thomas Carlyle wrote, "It is the Age of Machinery, in every outward and inward sense of the word."[4]

Thomas Carlyle (1795–1881) was one of the harshest critics of his age. Materialism and money worship shocked him; he opposed utilitarianism; he sympathized with the poor, the "slaves of industry," as he called them; and he attacked middle-class sham and hypocrisy, "proclaiming woe like an Old Testament prophet."[5] He directly attacked the political blindness and mediocrity of his age in *Past and Present* and opposed democracy in *Shooting Niagara—and After.* Besides writing political criticism, Carlyle lectured on heroes, wrote the classic history of the French Revolution, and produced a biography of Puritan political leader Oliver Cromwell.

Carlyle's opinions on Victorian society particularly influenced John Ruskin (1819–1900), who had spent much of his career as an art critic, writing *Modern Painters* and *The Seven Lamps of Architecture*. Ruskin turned to social issues when he realized that great art can flourish only in a good moral and social environment and that the conditions of his own times were faulty. John D. Cooke and Lionel Stevenson explain the relationship Ruskin saw between art and society:

> Industrialism, mass-production, city slums, were symptoms of an existence without love, joy, or self-respect. Therefore [Ruskin's] aesthetic philosophy suddenly became a dynamic social theory, in opposition to both the laissez-faire of current economics and the materialism of current science. The inevitable consequence of his new doctrine was a search for ways to remodel society in the direction of a beautiful and meaningful life for all.[6]

Ruskin delivered public lectures on his theories and published *A Joy Forever: The Political Economy of Art* in 1857.

Other nonfiction prose writers also commented on the rise of industrialism, each with his own slant on the subject. William Morris (1834–1896), for example, a skilled designer of pottery, glass, furniture, wallpaper, and fabrics, was disgusted by the glut of "things" industry could produce, most of which he believed were ugly, purposeless, or impractical. Refusing to believe that ordinary people were content with "cheap rubbish," he urged them to remove the clutter. In his writing he proclaimed, "We should have nothing in our homes that we do not know to be useful or believe to be beautiful."[7] Thomas Babington Macaulay (1800–1859), on the other hand, expressed an optimistic enthusiasm for individualism and for the material advantages the industrial age provided.

As these writers fulfilled their calling as prophets of the age, they never lost sight of their role as literary artists. They used wit and humor as weapons in their crusade. They presented multiple sides to a topic or an argument, as if they wanted to involve the reader in the fullness of the debate. However, passionately absorbed in their arguments, many of these writers produced long and convoluted works demanding a great deal of reading skill and patience from their audience.

SCIENCE CHALLENGES RELIGIOUS BELIEFS

Besides disruptive economic, social, and political changes, Victorians were confronted with a profound challenge to their religious beliefs, resulting from the publication of scientific findings. In 1830 Charles Lyell published *Principles of Geology*, in which he reported that layers of rock formations spanned long periods of time and showed that the earth was likely formed around 1,000,000,000 B.C. For Christians who believed in a static universe created by God on October 23, 4004 B.C., this discovery brought confusion and loss. In 1859 Charles Darwin published *Origin of Species,* which reported that species evolve by a process of natural selection. According to this theory, only the strongest individuals survive to form new species, and those unequal to the struggle die out. Darwin presented a persuasive case that all forms of life had in one way or another evolved from a primordial form and had continued to evolve by natural selection. In their anthology to English literature, Hazelton Spencer et al. imagine the effect of Darwin's theory on Victorian believers:

> In one terrible blow it seemed to destroy the traditional conceptions of man, of nature, and of the origin of religion and morality; and to substitute for each an interpretation that was deeply distressing. Man was reduced to an animal, the descendant of apes. Nature, which had been the witness of a divine and beneficent God and a source of moral elevation, became a battlefield in which individuals and species alike fought for their lives, and the victor was the best, not morally but physically, the toughest and the roughest.[8]

Victorians responded to this scientific challenge in various ways: denying that the scientific information was true, changing the emphases in their religion, embracing agnosticism, distracting themselves in work, or continually searching for some reconciliation between science and religion. Yet overall, the effect was gradually to unseat the authority of the church in many aspects of Victorian life.

THE NEW PRIESTHOOD

In such an unsettling atmosphere the Victorian public, trying to make sense of their world, searched for advisers they could trust to explain ideas, interpret events, and find threads of continuity. Hazelton Spencer says that the writer was most qualified to interpret life in new and fresh ways:

> It was [the writer's] natural task in an age of radical transition, when the Church and the aristocracy had lost their traditional authority, when the most fundamental questions in politics and religion cried out for new answers, and men were in need of guidance and inspiration.[9]

Essayists, historians, poets, and novelists took up the task, some unwittingly, some willingly, and some because they felt it was a duty thrust upon them. Thomas Carlyle believed that in the absence of other authority, a writer's job was to serve as moral guide. In a lecture in 1840, he said that there is in the true literary man "a sacredness; he is the light of the world; the world's Priest;—guiding it, like a sacred Pillar of Fire, in its dark pilgrimage through the waste of Time."[10] Writers gained a reputation as prophets and were referred to as a "priesthood." They were regularly sought as lecturers and after-dinner speakers, and their words even were used as guiding texts for sermons.

THE POETS AND THEIR SECLUSION

As much as Victorians emanated a sense of reserve and order, putting their faith in anyone or anything that could give them stability and purpose, the foundations of the past (in religion, in politics, in class distinctions) were eroding. In 1879 poet and essayist Matthew Arnold noted in his preface to *The Hundred Greatest Men,* "There is not a creed which is not shaken, not an accredited dogma which is not shown to be questionable, not a received tradition which does not threaten to dissolve."[11] Unlike the essayists of the time, Victorian poets tended to withdraw from these social concerns. They felt themselves incapable of dealing with the confusion of modern life; as critic and historian Margaret Drabble points out, they held "that poetry properly deals with specifically poetic and elevated themes, rather than with immediate reality."[12]

Many early Victorian poets shied away from the duty to furnish instruction. As a result their poetry tends to be nostalgic and escapist. Poets looked for historical subjects from classical and medieval literature, "closing their eyes to the smoke and squalor around them."[13] They longed for the beauty that had vanished from their mechanized world. Early in the Victorian period, poets preferred old literary forms; they wrote about trees and flowers, exemplified in Alfred, Lord Tennyson's "Flower in a Crannied Wall," and they created a dreamy world lulled by poetic rhythms, where, as Tennyson writes:

> The woods decay, the woods decay and fall,
> The vapours weep their burthen to the ground,
> Man comes and tills the field and lies beneath,
> And after many a summer dies the swan.[14]

Tennyson (1809–1892) was the most prolific and arguably most important Victorian poet. He was appointed poet laureate in 1850. In his early poems Tennyson languished in images of nature—mountains, flowers, birds, and often the sea—and populated his landscapes with past heroes such as Ulysses and legendary personages such as the title character in "The Lady of Shalott." His favorite period to invoke in his poetry was the age of chivalry and courtly romance, the subject of his twelve-volume *Idylls of the King*.

Robert Browning (1812–1889) expressed a rather optimistic view of Christianity in his poetry. Though not given to Christian orthodoxy, Browning adhered to Christian morality and his art reflects it. He found great excitement in tracing the inner workings of the human soul in his poems. His characters are often studies in human motives, for motives entail a weighing of personal desire against ethical consequences, and Browning was fascinated by the moral struggle. His tone is rough, eccentric, and often obscure, which sometimes distanced him from his audience. Browning was briefly exposed to theater writing, and the experience affected his poetry. His resulting dramatic monologues are well known for their structure and the psychological intricacies of their characters.

Another group of poets and artists withdrew from the confusion caused by political and religious changes and gave all of their attention to the aesthetic imagination. The Pre-Raphaelites declared "art for art's sake," indicating that they felt no compulsion to use their art as a vehicle for social commentary. Dante Gabriel Rossetti (1828–1882), both a painter and a poet, was the leader of this small movement. The Pre-Raphaelites made truth in nature as they saw it their highest priority, even if that truth was sometimes sinister rather than beautiful.

FACING THE CHANGING WORLD

The desire to avoid social commentary in the works of Tennyson, Browning, and other early Victorians was apparent. According to Margaret Drabble, "Reading through the *Oxford Book of Victorian Verse*, one might well imagine that its poets were . . . locked under some strong enchantment, from which some would from time to time struggle to escape."[15] The poets soon recognized, however, that the reading public was turning to prose, and attempted to draw on contemporary topics and the real world in their poetry. Tennyson, for example, made a serious effort to assimilate science, philosophy, and religion into his later poetry. In his long and involved poem, *In Memoriam* (commemorating the death of his friend Arthur Henry Hallam), Tennyson confronted the loss not only of a friend but of unshakable religious faith and other traditional sources of order that the new age was calling into question. "In Memoriam" was Tennyson's attempt to define the place of a poet in the changing world.

Like Tennyson, Matthew Arnold (1822–1888) was concerned with the religious doubt of his age, but he approached the issue from an intellectual more than emotional perspective. Arnold, unable to dismiss the loss he suffered from the lack of religious certainty, addressed this theme with intellectual passion in several poems. Literary critic Jerome Hamilton Buckley claims Arnold "taught in verse and prose the value of detached rational control and the danger of unleashed subjective emotion."[16]

Arnold had a deep concern for civilization, but he was unable to find solutions for the problems of his times. Whenever he returned to this theme, he expressed it in a tone of frustration. "Dover Beach," perhaps Arnold's finest poem, is an honest admission of his failure to find faith, his dignified and sad farewell to God. In it the speaker and his love stand on a "darkling plain" amid clashing, ignorant armies and "confused alarums of struggle and flight." The world that seemed full of new, varied, and beautiful dreams turned out to have nothing of joy, love, light, certitude, peace, or comfort. In the 1850s Arnold turned from writing poetry to a career in criticism and prose.

CHANGE IN TIMES, CHANGE IN FORMS

Not only did the confusion of the times affect the themes of Victorian poets, it also affected poetic form. Absent are the forms that evolve from a confident, courageous period—tragedy, epic, ballad, and the fixed lyric forms. Victorian poets tried to make the content of a poem determine its appropriate form, a new technique. Robert Browning's wife, Elizabeth Barrett Browning (1806–1861), wrote *Aurora Leigh*, called by some critics a novel in verse. Popular in its day, it is a passionately spoken amalgam of plots, commentary on social problems, romance, and ideas. Her other important work is a book of sonnets, another form seldom used by other Victorian poets. *Sonnets from the Portuguese* is the collection of love poems she wrote to Robert Browning during their courtship.

VICTORIAN FICTION

Victorian novelists had clearer direction than the poets; fiction writers rushed eagerly into topics that poets hesitated to consider. In reviewing the great number and varieties of novels of the period, Michael Wheeler states that "the Victorian novel reflects the energy and vitality of the age that witnessed more rapid and disturbing social and intellectual change than any other period before or since."[17] Forty thousand novels written during Victoria's reign presented the real world to a reading public eager to read. Not yet considered a serious art form, the novel grew in an unwieldy, unplanned fashion with no theory or rules to discipline it. Margaret Drabble says that Victorian novels were like the Victorian cities, "crowded, bursting with energy, often untidy and unplanned, a strange mixture of beauty and squalor, of high life and low life."[18] Readers liked them because they found familiar faces in the host of comic, criminal, pathetic, destitute, or wealthy characters going about their ordinary business.

Victorian novelists realistically documented social changes. Even in romantic fiction, writers included social, political, or religious themes. Social themes focused on conflict: between classes, between master and worker, between male seducer and female victim, between the individual and society, or between any combination of those elements. One recurring political theme explored how the turmoil in society caused a conflict between the inner life of feeling and the outer world of action, between an individual's will and socially determined factors like heredity, class, and environment. Another portrayed industrial society as physical, psychological, and spiritual imprisonment. Novels with religious themes depicted the strife among religious sects and the confusion and problems deriving from the challenges to orthodox belief. Historical novels presented history in terms of great heroes or as an examination of the past in order to entertain and teach the present generation.

DICKENS AND THACKERAY

Charles Dickens (1812–1870) was the most popular and the most prolific of the Victorian novelists. He wrote primarily about the lower classes, where he thought the most interesting and worthwhile people were found; he drew on his ex-

periences as a poor boy on the London streets and as a
worker in an ink-blacking factory. His tone was both realistic and romantic. That is, he portrayed life as it was, but he
sweetened bleak subjects with humor and sentiment, and he
exaggerated both beauty and ugliness. Within his many novels, he managed to cover the chief injustices of his age.
Bernard Grebanier et al. explain Dickens's role as a reformer:

> Most of his books attack some social evil: *Nicolas Nickleby*,
> the private schools; *The Old Curiosity Shop*, child labor; *Bleak
> House*, the cumbersome workings of the law; *Dombey and
> Son*, the egotism of the capitalist; *Oliver Twist*, the workhouse
> system; and so on. . . . [In *Hard Times*] the whole immorality
> of what he called "Gradgrind" economics [*i.e., laissez-faire*] is
> indicated, as may be seen by this passage: "It was a fundamental principle of the Gradgrind philosophy that everything
> was to be paid for. Nobody was ever on any account to give
> anybody anything, or render anybody help without purchase.
> . . . Every inch of the existence of mankind, from birth to
> death, was to be a bargain across a counter."[19]

Dickens's plots were episodic and contrived, with hastily
worked-out endings. The success and charm of his work lie
in the pictorial detail of his scenes and the memorable characters that people the novels. Robert Morss Lovett and Helen
Sard Hughes sum up his contribution to the world of letters:

> Dickens's world is not the best of all possible worlds, but it is
> one in which shadow makes sunshine the brighter. It is a
> world which in spite of its incredible phenomena is life-like
> in that it is alive, alive in its sorrow and its joy. . . . It was indeed as the universal entertainer of the English reading public that Dickens found his chief social importance.[20]

Like Dickens, William Makepeace Thackeray (1811–1863)
accepted his broad social responsibility to comment on his
society. But unlike Dickens, he held a mirror up to the
wealthy and the upper classes, writing less as a crusader and
more as a realist and satirist. His characters belong to the
real school—no perfect characters, no downright villains. He
made subtle war against pretension and selfishness, and he
sneered at the shallowness of popular ideals and sentiments.
Lovett and Hughes say of him:

> Thackeray makes more pitiful the sorrows of men and
> women, weak, stupid, sinful, absurd, whose sufferings result
> either from their own failings or from the evils of the world
> into which they have been born. This world Thackeray views
> with melancholy tempered by humor.[21]

Thackeray's best-known novel is *Vanity Fair,* a panoramic history of early-nineteenth-century England, in which he portrays the effect of money in the new society. He introduces this satire as a puppet show begging the reader to pay attention to his dolls. One of the puppets, Becky Sharp, is likable in spite of her dishonesty and another, Amellia Sedley, is as sweet and pure as she is stupid and selfish. This novel exemplifies Thackeray's style in that he ridicules the egotism and frustration of society while maintaining a tone of sympathy for his characters.

WOMEN NOVELISTS

The Brontë sisters, Charlotte and Emily, ignoring the social roles taken by Dickens and Thackeray, wrote novels about love. Out of frustration more than protest, both created passionate, independent women characters and wrote with a feminist tone that departed from Victorian ideals concerning women. In 1847 Charlotte (1816–1855) published *Jane Eyre,* her best-known novel. The story tells of Jane's search for friendship and love. The novel shocked Victorians because it addresses elemental psychological forces that control passion. There are no direct references to sex, but intense sexual love is clearly though subtly conveyed. Avoiding sentiment, *Jane Eyre* is a realistic novel in that Brontë presents love as human, not ideal. Emily Brontë (1818–1848) wrote one novel, *Wuthering Heights,* published in 1847. A novel unlike any other Victorian novel, it is a strange and mysterious love story of Catherine and Heathcliff, whose peculiarities of character border on madness. Catherine's spirit is influenced by the supernatural, and Heathcliff's character contains elements of satanic cruelty and revenge. Critics have called it a poetic tragedy rather than a novel. George Tillotson says that "*Wuthering Heights* is the one English novel that stands within hailing distance of *King Lear* and *Macbeth*."[22]

George Eliot, pseudonym for Mary Ann Evans (1819–1880), is recognized by critics as the most distinguished Victorian novelist because her work marks the high point in English realism. She was a progressive thinker and wrote about women as victims in a patriarchal society and about their need for education and useful employment. An intellectual with a scientific curiosity about human nature and psychology, Eliot depicts characters in actions that arise from their personalities and their motives. She was first a moralist, but she interjected into her morals her skepticism of traditional Christian beliefs, a desire for improvement and progress, and a respect for the past. Because she felt strongly about recording the life of the English countryside of her native Warwickshire before it changed beyond recognition, she drew on its beauty and native millers, carpenters, and tinkers for details in her early novels. Three novels—*Adam Bede, The Mill on the Floss,* and *Silas Marner*—depict Warwickshire. In her later works Eliot became more ambitious in experimenting with the art form. In *Middlemarch,* considered one of the greatest English novels, she begins with separate strands of narrative and skillfully weaves them into a single story about the effects of social change on provincial England.

MAGAZINES AND NEWSPAPERS

The vast number of Victorian novels would not have been written without a corresponding expansion of the reading public. Novels had traditionally been published in three volumes, but as lower-class readers became more numerous, publishers made novels more affordable by serializing them in smaller parts. In addition, literary magazines and other periodicals began including chapters of novels within their pages, subsequently drawing large readerships. In 1860 Thackeray started the magazine *Cornhill,* in the first issue of which he published the first chapters of one of his novels and one by Anthony Trollope. It sold 110,000 copies at a shilling apiece.

Novels, serial magazines, and newspapers—which were responsible for much adult education—suited an increasingly urban English society. In 1841, 48 percent of the population lived in cities and towns; by 1880 over 70 percent did, making it easy to distribute magazines and newspapers. In 1815 England had 250 newspapers that each sold 2,000 copies; in 1875 there were 1,600 that sold two hundred and fifty thousand. There were publications for varied tastes: Some were limited to serious nonfiction sought by the public for education; others offered entertainment and guidance suitable for family reading; still others offered escapist fiction with criminals and rogues as characters, improbable plots, and reckless heroes. In a society without television or radio and with the challenge of a changing way of life, the Victorian public had a great desire to read, and writers and publishers accommodated them.

LATE VICTORIAN LITERATURE

By the 1880s reforms enacted by Parliament had taken effect and society had begun to change again. Literature, of course, followed suit. Emerging late Victorian novelists reacted against the seriousness of fiction and challenged the notion that writers had a duty to be moral teachers. New writers considered the novel an opportunity to convey fresh ideas and more modern points of view. In the waning years of the century, strong voices expressed both pessimism and optimism at the progressively secular and materialistic age.

Poet and novelist Thomas Hardy (1840–1928) possessed a pessimistic outlook. Like Matthew Arnold, Hardy was perplexed by the scientific discoveries that seemed to dethrone God. Because he could not accept the loss of his childhood God, he reasoned that perhaps God exists but is indifferent toward humans, generating a profound sense of alienation.

Hardy's novels frequently caused controversy in his own time because he treated human passion and sexuality too openly for Victorian tastes. Moreover, they challenged the reader because he used his novels to debate ethical and philosophical uncertainty rather than simply to entertain and teach correct moral attitudes. His novels create the world as a dark place, cold and desolate, full of accident and tragedy. His characters, despite their flaws, misjudgments, virtues, good intentions, or hard work, are ultimately controlled by chance. These themes prevail, for example, in *The Return of the Native, The Mayor of Casterbridge, Tess of the D'Urbervilles,* and *Jude the Obscure.*

Other late Victorian writers had more optimistic attitudes. Rudyard Kipling (1865–1936) wrote short stories and poems often expressing his loyalty to his country and the glory of the expanding British empire. He was so taken with progress that, at the end of the century, he advocated a new poetry to celebrate the beauty of the machine. He is best remembered, however, for his romantic novels and stories such as *The Jungle Book* and *Captains Courageous.* Robert Louis Stevenson (1850–1894), essayist, poet, and novelist, also wrote adventurous, imaginative fiction at a time when many writers were mired in serious realism. He optimistically displays his courageous personal philosophy and his love of life in novels such as *Treasure Island, Dr. Jekyll and Mr. Hyde,* and *Kidnapped.* Furthermore, the novels of H.G.

Wells (1866–1946) illustrate the importance that new scientific knowledge had on literature and the growth of science fiction as a genre. The romance of the machine and of adventure are depicted in *The Time Machine, The Invisible Man,* and *War of the Worlds.* These writers represent a return to optimism and romance in contrast to many of their colleagues who saw the world beset by moral indifference and social ills.

LOOKING TO THE PAST AND TO THE FUTURE

At the close of Victoria's reign and the dawn of a new century, a retrospective review shows a literature that began in romanticism and ended primarily in realism. It was a literature that recorded great change and struggle in British society. Bernard Grebanier offers this summation of the period:

> In versatility these writers probably exceeded those of the generation immediately before them. If they did not produce equally high examples of excellence, we can now understand better than they could the threats that hung over them. In sum, they lived only a little on the fair-weather side of the deluge that was about to break.[25]

The great deluge was World War I. Though they could not know why, the pessimists came closer than the optimists in anticipating the future, in sensing that their lives hung in tragic imbalance soon to be jarred by a great catastrophe. In the new century, the modernists would record its effects in their poems and novels.

NOTES

1. Quoted in Jerome Hamilton Buckley, *The Victorian Temper: A Study in Literary Culture.* Cambridge, MA: Harvard University Press, 1951, p. 4.
2. Anthony Wood, *Nineteenth Century Britain: 1815–1914.* New York: David McKay, 1960, p. 256.
3. Robert Morss Lovett and Helen Sard Hughes, *The History of the Novel in England.* Boston: Houghton Mifflin, 1932, p. 186.
4. Quoted in Herbert L. Sussman, *Victorians and the Machine: The Literary Response to Technology.* Cambridge, MA: Harvard University Press, 1968, p. 6.
5. John D. Cooke and Lionel Stevenson, *English Literature of the Victorian Period.* New York: Appleton-Century-Crofts, 1949, p. 378.
6. Cooke and Stevenson, *English Literature,* p. 395.

7. Quoted in Margaret Drabble, *For Queen and Country*. New York: The Seabury Press, 1978, p. 108.

8. Hazelton Spencer et al., eds., *British Literature: 1800 to the Present*, vol. 2, 3rd ed. Lexington, MA: D.C. Heath, 1974, p. 419.

9. Spencer et al., *British Literature*, p. 424.

10. Quoted in George Tillotson, *A View of Victorian Literature*. Oxford: Clarendon Press, 1978, p. 11.

11. Quoted in Tillotson, *A View of Victorian Literature*, p. 8.

12. Drabble, *For Queen and Country*, p. 118.

13. Drabble, *For Queen and Country*, p. 118.

14. Quoted in Drabble, *For Queen and Country*, p. 116.

15. Drabble, *For Queen and Country*, p. 120.

16. Buckley, *The Victorian Temper*, pp. 26–27.

17. Michael Wheeler, *English Fiction of the Victorian Period, 1830–1890*, 2nd ed. New York: Longman, 1994, p. 13.

18. Drabble, *For Queen and Country*, p. 127.

19. Bernard D. Grebanier et al., eds., *English Literature and Its Backgrounds*, vol. 2, *From The Forerunners of Romanticism to the Present*. Rev. ed. New York: Dryden, 1949, p. 443

20. Lovett and Hughes, *The History of the Novel in England*, p. 236.

21. Lovett and Hughes, *The History of the Novel in England*, p. 269.

22. Tillotson, *A View of Victorian Literature*, p. 202.

23. Grebanier et al., *English Literature and Its Backgrounds*, p. 800.

CHAPTER 1

The Era
of Reform

Victorian
Literature

Victorian Writers Provided Public Guidance

Walter E. Houghton

Victorian society was in transition: The authority of the church and the aristocracy had broken down, and people were left without traditional moral and intellectual guidelines and inspiration. Walter E. Houghton explains how Victorian writers filled the void. Especially appropriate, according to Houghton, were essays published in periodicals, short pieces that told readers what to think and believe; at the same time poets and novelists provided inspiration, emotional support, and escape from their worries. After 1850, however, a group of artists and poets rejected a prophetic role and insisted that art—literature and painting—should exist for art's sake and not serve as reform or social guide. Walter E. Houghton taught English at Wellesley College in Massachusetts. He is the editor, with G. Robert Stange, of *Victorian Poetry and Poetics.*

If we compare the literature of the Victorian age with the literature that preceded it or followed it, in the Romantic or the Modern period, we are struck by its public character and its public importance. Of the great Romantic writers, only [Lord] Byron and [Walter] Scott were widely read, and essentially for entertainment. [William] Wordsworth, [Percy Bysshe] Shelley, [John] Keats, [William] Hazlitt, and [Charles] Lamb had each a following of devotees, but it was small. Moreover, although Romantic art sometimes dealt with contemporary political, economic, and religious problems, it did not center upon them nor did it handle them in a form likely to attract the general reader. . . .

On the whole, the situation [in the twentieth century] is

Excerpted from Walter E. Houghton, "The Victorian Period," in *British Literature, 1800 to the Present,* vol. 2, 3rd. ed. (Lexington, MA: D.C. Heath, 1974). Copyright 1952, 1963, 1974 by D.C. Heath and Company.

very similar. Modern literature is a "thing apart"—too eso-
teric in content, too subtle and difficult in form, to reach any
but a small audience of "intellectuals." The modern writer
has no status. It is not to him but to specialists, or journalists, that people turn for answers to the pressing problems of
our time. Only the novel on the level of entertainment commands a reading public of any size.

But between these two periods, for the fifty years from
1830 to 1880, literature was a living medium of culture. Because at its best it was in close touch with the general life of
the time and spoke in a language that was simple without
being flat or conventional, it commanded a wide audience.
And the prestige of the writer was little short of amazing. If
[Thomas] Carlyle's high claim that the Man of Letters was
"our most important modern person," possessed of intuitive
insight into "the True, Divine and Eternal," and therefore
"the light of the world, . . . guiding it, like a sacred Pillar of
Fire, in its dark pilgrimage" (a theory derived from the Romantic conception of the natural genius), if this was, at bottom, a counterdefiance hurled at Philistine[1] indifference and
a kind of self-sustaining boast, it came, nonetheless, to be
widely acknowledged not only by writers but by readers as
well. According to [John Stuart] Mill, Carlyle "made Artist
the term for expressing the highest order of moral and intellectual greatness."

Mill's choice of adjectives is significant. The public nature
and the public importance of Victorian literature rested precisely there, on its moral and intellectual character, and not
on its imaginative re-creation of life. The task of the writer,
as [Matthew] Arnold put it, was "not to exhibit all the king-
doms of human life and the glory of them like Shakespeare,
but to interpret human life afresh." It was his natural task in
an age of radical transition, when the Church and the aristocracy had lost their traditional authority, when the most
fundamental questions in politics and religion cried out for
new answers, and men were in need of guidance and inspiration. Under such conditions his inevitable role, as we see
plainly in Carlyle's Lecture V, "The Hero as Man of Letters,"
was that of a prophet. It was a platitude of Victorian criticism
that authors were a modern priesthood whose duty was to

---

1. a smug, ignorant, especially middle-class person, who is considered to be indifferent or antagonistic to artistic and cultural values

"enlighten and encourage and purify public opinion." The essential style of this prose was described by [essayist] Walter Bagehot in a revealing article called "The First Edinburgh Reviewers." The difference, he said, between ancient and modern writing of a philosophical kind was due to the fact that "we must instruct so many persons." So long as he wrote for a small group of educated men, the writer could be "systematic, suggesting all arguments, analyzing all difficulties, discussing all doubts"; but now that he must write for the multitude, "impatient of system, desirous of brevity, puzzled by formality," he had to give his ideas a simpler and shorter expression:

> In this transition from ancient writing to modern, the review-like essay and the essay-like review fill a large space. Their small bulk, their slight pretension to systematic completeness,—their avowal, it might be said, of necessary incompleteness—the facility of changing the subject, of selecting points to attack, of exposing only the best corner for defense, are great temptations. . . . Unquestionably the Spectator and Tatler,[2] and such like writings, had opened a similar vein; but their size was too small: they could only deal with small fragments or the extreme essence of a subject; they could not give a view of what was complicated, or analyze what was involved. The modern man must be told what to think; shortly, no doubt, but he must be told it. The essay-like criticism of modern times is about the length which he likes. The Edinburgh Review, which began the system, may be said to be, in this country, the commencement on large topics of suitable views for sensible persons.

THE IMPORTANCE OF PERIODICALS AND THEIR ESSAY FORM

The *Edinburgh Review* (Whig)[3] was followed by the *Quarterly* (Tory), the *Westminster* (Utilitarian), and scores of others. The Victorian period is the golden age of the periodical at its highest level, where it is a vehicle for the best intelligence of the time. As that would suggest, much of the work of [Thomas Babington] Macaulay and Arnold, Carlyle and Mill and [Thomas] Huxley, first appeared in the reviews. Some of their most famous books—Arnold's *Culture and Anarchy*, for example, and Huxley's *Science and the Christian Tradition*—were collections of essays reprinted from periodicals. Even whole books ([Carlyle's] *Past and Present* is a clear case) explore a range of loosely connected ideas in a series of essay-like chapters.

2. newspapers   3. Whig and Tory are political parties; Utilitarians subscribed to a pragmatic philosophy.

But the intellectual character of the age was as important as its democratic audience in making the essay a "natural" for the time. When there was no longer any accepted body of beliefs, and men were wrestling with a multitude of new facts and tentative theories, they saw truth in fragments— and wrote it in essays. Furthermore, the very limitation of length, which allowed the writer, as [Walter] Bagehot says, to avoid "analyzing all difficulties, discussing all doubts," was entirely welcome to a public which wanted solutions and not deeper—and more confusing—analysis.

This last point bears directly on style. At a time when doubt was painful and the will to believe intense, what people craved above all was to be told—and in no uncertain terms. They did not want balanced arguments in a cool and measured style. They wanted positive doctrine expressed with eloquent and dogmatic conviction. When Carlyle taught [essayist and historian James] Froude a creed which saved him from atheism, "the lesson came from one who seemed 'to speak with authority and not as the Scribes,' as if what he said was absolute certainty beyond question or cavil." Had it not been so, Froude might not have been saved. One critic excused [John] Ruskin's "arrogance and dogmatism" on the extraordinary ground that "even error, eloquently advocated with the honest conviction that it is truth, is better than truth coldly believed and languidly proclaimed"—extraordinary only if we forget that it was an age "at once destitute of faith and terrified at scepticism." For their part the prophets were not only willing to meet the public demand; they had their own good reasons for adopting the tone of authority. When each school of political or religious thought (often with its own periodical) was fighting its rivals, the sectarian spirit encouraged dogmatism [arrogant assertion of opinions]. When the prestige of intuition that marked the Romantic reaction against eighteenth-century rationalism was at its height, and the artist was endowed with an almost mystical power of insight, the writer might well substitute authoritative statement for logical argument. What [philosopher and writer Herbert] Spencer said of Carlyle could be applied to many, though not all, of the prose prophets: he "never set out from premises and reasoned his way to conclusions, but habitually dealt in intuitions and dogmatic assertions."

To speak more precisely, the prophets were men of letters

writing prophetic literature. Their prose has usually been thought of as ideas treated with rhetorical skill. But [since the 1950s], teachers and scholars have come to feel that the achievement of Carlyle, [John Henry] Newman, Arnold, and Ruskin—to mention only the greatest names—was the kind of thing they were accustomed to think of "as the peculiar activity of poets and novelists." In a novel we expect a series of incidents—linked by a plot—a cast of characters, dialogue or monologue (speaking voices), ideas and value judgments— explicit and implicit—pictures of places and scenery, and imagery—descriptive and figurative. When all the elements are fused, the result is a personal vision or reading of life which can only be described in shorthand. Compare a book like [Carlyle's] *Past and Present:* it has not only the life of the monastery with its sharply drawn monks, but also telling incidents, each centering on a character (Columbus on the voyage to America, rugged Brindly, John Bull, the poor Irish widow with typhus); there is not only dialogue but monologue as well, often in close conjunction with statements of political ideas and moral judgments; perhaps above all, there is vivid imagery.

> Our life is not a mutual helpfulness; but rather, cloaked under due laws-of-war, named "fair competition" and so forth, it is a mutual hostility. We have profoundly forgotten everywhere that Cash-payment is not the sole relation of human beings; we think, nothing doubting, that it absolves and liquidates all engagements of man. "My starving workers?" answers the rich Millowner: "Did not I hire them fairly in the market? Did I not pay them, to the last sixpence, the sum covenanted for? What have I to do with them more?"—Verily Mammon-Worship is a melancholy creed.

Surely this is the work of an artist; and taken as a symbol of the whole, it illustrates the literary forms of self-expression which create a Carlylean vision of England in 1843.

Between the prophetic literature of prose and that of poetry and fiction, one may make a rough distinction on the lines laid down by Carlyle. The former is intended to persuade, to affect public opinion; the latter to inspire, to affect the character. In the one case, doctrine is central; in the other, "noble sentiments," in the form of either moral reflections or ideal images—usually both at once. George Eliot felt that the function of the novelist was "that of the *aesthetic,* not the doctrinal teacher,—the rousing of the nobler emotions, which make mankind desire the social right, not the prescribing of special measures." For Arnold, the function of poetry in an age when traditional religion was dying was "to interpret life for us, to console us, to sustain us."

A PRIESTHOOD OF POETS INSPIRED READERS

This moral pressure on the artist was apparent in the 1830s, when a reaction against the verbal beauties of Shelley and Keats and the wild, passionate heroes of Byron called for a literature of "noble images and thoughts." [Alfred] Tennyson was forced to abandon his early romantic poetry of mood and impression to supply the age with moral reflections or heroic characters. [Robert] Browning, whose natural gift was for detached observation, was induced by Elizabeth Barrett[4] and the gospel of Carlyle to make some of his studies of men and women illustrations of moral aspiration. Though Arnold complained in 1849 that under the influence of Wordsworth verse had become "a channel for thinking aloud, instead of making anything," much of his own poetry is filled with moral reflection; or, when that is not the case, offers "some noble action of a heroic time" to inspire and sustain an anxious generation. And there is no doubt that the prophetic purpose was welcomed. In at least one Victorian home where the parents had been "emancipated" by reading [biologist Charles] Darwin and Huxley, and where no one mentioned the Bible or went to church, the children were brought up on the Greek pantheon and the Arthurian Round Table. In the living room hung a picture of Sir Galahad by Frederick Watts, with the quotation from Tennyson:

> *My strength is as the strength of ten,*
> *Because my heart is pure.*

On the library table was a finely bound copy of *The Poetical Works of Robert Browning* containing his modern version of chivalric love and his high doctrine of aspiration toward impossible goals:

> *'Tis not what man Does which exalts him, but what man Would do!*

In literal fact the Victorian poets became, as Carlyle predicted, a modern priesthood.

It must not be supposed that in itself a didactic intention[5] is fatal to a work of art; still less that poetry of noble images or moral reflection is bad poetry. Shakespeare and Milton may be cited at once to the contrary. The critical estimate de-

---

4. poet and wife of Robert Browning 5. to teach a moral lesson

pends on the treatment. The noble image must not be too noble; the hero must be a human being and not an idealized abstraction or a self-conscious preacher of his own virtues (like Galahad in the quotation from Tennyson just given). Moral reflections must be translated into music and image, not simply stated (as they might be in a treatise or a sermon, as they *are* in the line by Browning quoted above). They must be "experienced" by the sensibility of the artist, not merely "thought" by the mind. Or they must arise implicitly from the concrete presentation of character and action, instead of being explicitly injected. The Victorian record, in these respects, is varied. All one can say is that the strong demand of the age for high ideals and moral guidance made artistic success more difficult to achieve, though by no means impossible.

POETS OFFER ESCAPE AND EMOTIONAL EXPRESSION

Furthermore, these pressures were not always operative; and a considerable body of Victorian poetry is innocent of prophetic intention. By moments the poets turned away from the needs and problems of the time, and away from its "unpoetic" environment of dirt and smoke and cutthroat competition, to seek relief in some image of ideal beauty, of woods and flowers, of faraway places and olden times—ancient Greece or medieval England, the Orient or a land of lotos-eating. Side by side with the motive to instruct and inspire was the motive to escape. It is because the heroic image could satisfy both motives at once—and meet both desires in their readers—that the Victorian writers turned so often to the mythology of Greece and Scandinavia and the legends of a time when knighthood was in flower. It is highly significant that when Arnold told the poet to abandon thinking and writing about the problems of the age, he suggested that instead he ought "to delight himself with the contemplation of some noble action of a heroic time, and to enable others, through his representation of it, to delight in it also." You have your cake and eat it too—escape to the glamour of heroic adventure and feel the moral inspiration of a noble action. This double effect is produced by Arnold's "Sohrab and Rustum," Tennyson's *Idylls of the King,* [William] Morris's *Earthly Paradise*—and in prose by [Charles] Kingsley's *Heroes, or Greek Fairy Tales.*

But for all these distractions, a considerable body of Victorian verse is simply a record of living experience. In his

"Essay on Shelley" Browning described not only the subjective poet who searches his soul for divine wisdom, but also the objective poet who chooses to deal with "the noisy, complex, yet imperfect exhibitions of human nature in the manifold experience of man around him." Certainly many of Browning's men and women are sketched with psychological penetration. We may also remember that however inconsistent with other statements of his (the inconsistency is inevitable in a period of intellectual uncertainty), Arnold could also insist on a poetry that should "appeal to the great primary human affections: to those elementary feelings which subsist permanently in the race. . . ." Perhaps chief among these feelings at the time were those of dejection and despair, rising from the breakdown of traditional ideas and modes of life, and often accompanied by the sense of isolation, loneliness, and nostalgia. The more sensitive Victorians felt like displaced persons, cut off from a divine relationship, divided from families and friends by religious differences, and unwilling to enter the amoral world of industrial struggle. This is the creative background that lies behind the early poems of Tennyson and some of the finest lyrics of *In Memoriam;* Arnold's "Dover Beach," "The Scholar-Gipsy," "Stanzas from the Grande Chartreuse," and the second "Isolation: To Marguerite"; most of the poetry of [Arthur] Clough; and nearly all of that of [Thomas] Hardy. Because we [in the twentieth century] ourselves are also caught in the same world, or a worse one, we find that these expressions of anxiety and loneliness speak to us with immediacy.

THE PRE-RAPHAELITES AND ART FOR ART'S SAKE

Starting in the 1850s the Pre-Raphaelites ([Christina and Dante Gabriel] Rossetti, Morris, and [Algernon Charles] Swinburne were the chief poets) inaugurated a movement that later evolved into the Aesthetes and Decadents of the nineties (Oscar Wilde and the early [William Butler] Yeats), with Walter Pater as chief philosopher-critic. Among these men there was considerable diversity of opinion and practice, but they all agreed on one thing, that it was *not* the business of art to instruct or inspire, nor the function of an artist to be a prophet. Art, as the battle cry put it, was for art's sake, and an artist—was an artist. But what did this mean, in theory and in fact? The various answers are implicit in Morris's lecture on Pre-Raphaelitism.

The Aesthetic Movement began in 1848 when a new and radical group of painters, who called themselves Pre-Raphaelites, first exhibited their pictures. What was radical was their insistence that an artist should paint what he saw regardless of the traditional "rules" of painting. In technical terms they were Naturalists: they were imitating nature as they experienced it directly instead of nature as it had been portrayed by earlier painters; and they were painting "naturally," in forms and colors faithful to their experience, not in those which had come down in the art schools of Europe since the Renaissance as the "right" techniques. . . .

In short, Pre-Raphaelitism was a return, not to the form and style of early Italian painting, but to its freedom from the requirement of painting ideal figures according to the rules that Raphael had laid down. As Morris points out, the same revolt had occurred fifty years earlier in literature when Wordsworth and [Samuel Taylor] Coleridge had led the reaction against neoclassical conventions in poetry and had set up the contrary aim of keeping the eye on the object, that is, imitating nature as they saw it—which explains why Ruskin can say that "the Pre-Raphaelite school was headed, in literary power, by Wordsworth." In origin, therefore, the Aesthetic Movement was not antididactic: it was antiacademic. But the primary insistence on fidelity to experience was, in effect, a rejection of the prophetic principle.

Victorian Writers Rejected Radical Social Reforms

Roland A. Duerksen

Roland A. Duerksen clarifies the position of major Victorian writers by explaining their reaction to Romantic poet Percy Bysshe Shelley's reform ideas, which asserted that individuals should use their freedoms more effectively and, thus, transform society gradually and peacefully toward greater democracy and a better future. According to Duerksen, most Victorian writers either misunderstood Shelley's ideas, thinking that Shelley meant instant and total reform when indeed he called for gradual, peaceful change, or they rejected his ideas in favor of traditional social institutions. Roland A. Duerksen is Professor Emeritus at Miami University of Ohio. He has contributed articles to the *Victorian Newsletter*, the *Keats-Shelley Journal,* and the *PMLA,* the Publication of the Modern Language Association.

[Percy Bysshe] Shelley's social ideas presented the Victorian thinkers with a serious dilemma. The demand of these ideas was that an individual or a society must be willing to discard tradition and disregard the status quo whenever a conviction of truth indicated the need for such an abandonment. In the early years of Victoria's reign there was an unprecedented urge and impetus toward a radical revision of numerous long-accepted social standards. The industrial revolution had pervaded all of England and had left its aftermath, the need for social readjustment, as the great problem for Victorians to solve. Shelley . . . had found the old standards, mores, and beliefs inadequate; he had insisted upon a conscious and incessant progression toward a society founded upon new, more logical and truthful principles. The natural inclination of society, however, was to hold tenaciously to the old traditions and institutions as the framework which, if it must be altered or extended in its various parts, was yet capable of comprehending whatever changes the new way of life might bring. Thoughtful writers of the time were torn between the challenge of Shelley's intellectual honesty and the security offered by the predominant conservative reaction in their own age.

Those who, in the days of the first Reform Act[1] and of Chartism,[2] were inspired by the Shelleyan ideas to commit themselves to progress toward a new social order, soon found its demands more stringent than they had anticipated. [Robert] Browning, despite a basic affinity with Shelley's spirit, could not break with family loyalties and a longing for the old religious assurances. He abandoned what was essentially Shelleyan in his philosophy to half-heartedly re-endorse the religiosity exemplified to him by the chapel of the Dissenters.[3] [Writer and politician Benjamin] Disraeli's defection from his early response to the liberalizing influence of Shelley came about through his official political involvements which demanded the conservative approach. And [historian and writer Charles] Kingsley, much as he was drawn to Shelley and freely though he criticized aspects of the Church of England, found that his commitment to traditional religion required a complete rejection of Shelleyan principles. The literary work of these representative early Victorians is a reflection of their era, an age facing the challenging need for a new and creative social view but not daring to progress toward it beyond a point of no return.

This lack of venturesomeness had the result which might be expected: a concerted effort to reassert old values and to strengthen traditional institutions. The effort was immensely successful for some decades, and perhaps no period in English history has been more complacent and ostensibly more successful than the 1850's, 60's, and 70's. The response of the mid-Victorian writers to Shelleyan ideas was also what might be expected. Almost without exception, they either denounced Shelley as "mad" or pictured him as a lovely but impractical poet of beauty. [Thomas] Carlyle and

---

1. The first Reform Act, passed in 1832, enfranchised middle-class merchants, manufacturers, professionals, and tradespeople. Each of the three Reform Acts extended the vote to a larger segment of the population.   2. a working-class movement, 1838–1848, to extend franchise   3. Protestant groups who broke with the Church of England

[Alfred] Tennyson, respectively, were the forerunners of these two mid-Victorian opinions. Carlyle's aversion to Shelley's "shrieking" found a large following; but Tennyson's detection of "a sort of tenuity" in Shelley's poetry became representative of the more typical view. Matthew Arnold, although a fellow-spirit with Shelley, insofar as he realized the inadequacy of the old answers, chose to emphasize the Tennysonian view and to proclaim a tradition in which he himself no longer believed. And Arnold's judgment of Shelley, declaring him absurdly ineffectual, has survived the efforts of scholars such as William Michael Rossetti and of the Shelley Society to combat it, and has remained a prominent one to our day.

The author who, during the mid-Victorian period, came out most decisively in favor of Shelley was George Eliot; and her comment on him is limited to the presentation of one character—Ladislaw in *Middlemarch*. No doubt, it was her consort, G.H. Lewes, an admirer of Shelley, who acquainted her with the Shelleyan socio-political views attributed to Ladislaw. In general, writers of the period appear to have been determined not to take Shelley's ideas seriously but rather to think of him as a mere visionary and dispenser of lovely verses. [Minor poet] Thomas Wade's lines about Shelley,

> I have heard thee *Dreamer* styled—
> I've mused upon their wakefulness—and smiled,

appear to be more applicable to this period than to the earlier time in which they were written.

The new seriousness with which Shelley was viewed in the later Victorian era is evident in the works of [William] Morris, [George] Gissing, [Thomas] Hardy, and [William Butler] Yeats. Of these writers, Morris was least in accord with Shelley's ideas about the actual future of mankind, and Yeats appears to have misinterpreted their basic tenet—therefore, coming to regret the extent to which Shelley had influenced him. Gissing and Hardy both give evidence of a greater accord with Shelleyan ideas than the usual evaluations of their work indicate. Of all the Victorians, however, [playwright] George Bernard Shaw understood Shelley best and applied his ideas most consistently.

The beliefs which Shaw clearly derived from Shelley, and by which many other Victorians were challenged, are concerned largely with an optimism about humankind's ability to make for itself a better future. The emphasis is upon the necessity of changing the nature and the thought patterns of mankind, of achieving social—not merely political—reform. Shelley was thoroughly opposed to the old class structure of society and was enthusiastic about the growing ascendancy of the working people. His proposal was not, however, that one ruling class should be substituted for another; it was rather that the individual be taught to make profitable use of all the freedom of which he is capable. The problem which Victorians almost invariably found in this proposal was that it did away with the comfortable rules by which, for many years, the accepted conventions and institutions had governed English society. Gissing and Hardy were willing to try a way of life without these old rules, but it was Shaw who set forth a positive program based on the new concepts which Shelley had advocated.

In view of the apocalyptic[4] tone of *Prometheus Unbound*, the extreme social innovations proposed in *The Revolt of Islam*, and the immaturity of thought apparent in *Queen Mab*, the Victorians may perhaps be partially excused for their failure to comprehend Shelley's basic purposes. *The Philosophical View of Reform* having remained unpublished, they . . . could not believe Shelley capable of practical political and social analysis. It was easy to accept the popular, and most erroneous, conception of Shelley as a believer in an instantaneous transformation of society as the result of a sudden change in man's thinking. It was very difficult to grasp his belief in slow, gradual, but persistent progress. One of his most important precepts—that the approach to a peaceful society must itself be peaceful—was thus largely unheeded. As twentieth-century history and the present-day world situation testify—with a few notable exceptions, such as Gandhi's effort in India and the more recent nonviolent movement conducted by American Negroes—it has remained consistently unheeded.

We may regret that the Victorians either did not rightly understand or did not wish to accept Shelley and may conjecture about the difference which a better insight into his philosophy would have made in twentieth-century literature and life. We may be amazed at the reiteration by the aging Yeats, as late as 1933, of the old misconception about Shelley's prophetic view. And we must acknowledge the unique-

---

4. portending widespread devastation or ultimate doom

ness of Shaw, whose youthful understanding of Shelley appears to have changed only in that its agreement with his own interpretation of life became increasingly apparent. But what we cannot help but find astonishing is the fact that the present-day popular conception of Shelley, despite the high regard for Shaw's works, the publication of *A Philosophical View*, and the availability of a quantity of subsequent, enlightened criticism, has progressed but slightly beyond Matthew Arnold's portrayal of an "ineffectual angel".

Victorian Essayists Criticized the Industrial Age

Edith C. Batho and Bonamy Dobrée

Edith C. Batho and Bonamy Dobrée analyze the criticism of major Victorian prose writers. Macaulay, the exception, writes charming readable essays more in support of the Victorian age than against it. In contrast, according to the authors, Carlyle, Ruskin, Arnold, and Morris harshly criticize the economics of the industrial revolution for its disregard of the working poor, for its degrading attitude toward the individual, and for its lack of taste in art and beauty. Edith C. Batho, who was principal of Royal Holloway College, University of London, is the author of *The Later Wordsworth* and *The Poet and the Past*. Bonamy Dobrée, who taught English at the University of Leeds, is the author of *Restoration Comedy, 1660–1720* and *Essays in Biography*.

[Thomas Babington] Macaulay's clangorous prose and shallow thoughts moulded men's ideas for three-quarters of a century. He stamped the Whig [political] idea on three generations. It is not our business here to discuss the rightness or wrongness of his doctrine, nor to examine his historical accuracy, but to discuss his literary claims and his place in the story of our era. His literary merits are obvious, they even advertise themselves. His prose flows along vigorously, it is well-balanced, and free from any ambiguity; but indeed there is no excuse for a man not to be clear when he has no doubts as to the rightness of his thoughts. His essays are robust, full of common sense and crammed with information; he was always able to bring an amazing amount of knowledge to bear upon any point that occurred to him. His judgment of persons is never subtle, and his appraisal of literary

Excerpted from Edith C. Batho and Bonamy Dobrée, *The Victorians and After, 1830–1914* (London: Cresset Press, 1938).

points is so "sound" as often to be almost meaningless; yet he is not always trite, and though he is so often wrong about the details of people's lives, he has an uncanny trick of getting the general perspective right; time has reversed the "soundness" of his literary views, yet they have acquired a meaning as representing something of his age. He was the first to write history that everybody could read; he had a most unusual talent for narrative, and besides could bring his readers into close touch with the daily lives of people in the past. His description of England at the end of the seventeenth century is an acknowledged masterpiece which combines movement and vividness with compression. But he could never see anything except through the eyes of a thoroughly representative and highly successful early nineteenth-century bureaucrat; his prose, for all its skill, is a machine-made product of the industrial revolution; it works beautifully, like a well-oiled engine; it glitters magnificently as the pistons work smoothly and relentlessly up and down. No one can help admiring Macaulay. He was as near being an artist as a man can be who has nothing of the artist in him. The *Essays* are overwhelmingly brilliant; the *History* is a shattering achievement; but they are just not the real thing, in the same way as *Lays of Ancient Rome* are just not real poetry. But Macaulay exists as an immaculately representative figure.

What he represented was a very important, perhaps the dominant, side of early Victorianism. He shared the opacity of vision combined with a certain grandeur, a certain nobility even. He shared also the complacency, but with him it was hard, not soft. He believed in God and he believed in the British Constitution; both were perfect, and existed for the sake of Britons; but the Constitution had been created by good Whigs in a hundred hard-fought battles. He represented, in fact, just those sides of the early-Victorian mind, which, enormously useful as they undoubtedly were, we have come to hate, though perhaps we might be grateful if we could share its certitude. The curious thing about Macaulay is that, distinguished man of letters that he was, he was the only one who thought as he did and still remains great. The others have sunk into derision, or maintain a lesser place by reason of other qualities (Sir James Stephen, for example). Everybody who still retains eminence fought hard against those very things for which he stood so placidly, and, it would seem, unconsciously. Opposed to him on all the grand points are the great men who, in the sphere of literature, walked as giants in those and immediately succeeding days: [Thomas] Carlyle, [John] Ruskin, [Matthew] Arnold, [William] Morris.

They make an odd quartette; the dyspeptic Scotch peasant, the neurotic rich wine-merchant's son, the correct product of Rugby and Oxford,[1] and the giant who radiated health from his heart, his hands, and his head. They were all tremendous—yes, even Arnold—they were temperamentally antagonistic on many points, and they drew quite different results from similar causes. . . .

But there is no end to the curiosities we discover if we try to unravel the threads of cultural heredity in this exciting and confused age. The important thing to notice is that all four of these men hated as the thing above all things accurst the prevalent philosophy of economics which the industrial revolution, together with Adam Smith, [Jeremy] Bentham, the Mills [James and John Stuart] and others had brought about. They all fought it tooth and nail, for different reasons, and with different remedies in view; they fought it in various ways, by screaming, by preaching, by reasoning, by doing; and though they do not seem to have had any great immediate effect, their efforts probably prevented things from being as bad as they might have been, and they planted seeds which are only now, it would seem, beginning to sprout. Arnold is the exception; his seed came up too soon, and the visible harvest is over; yet what he stood for will necessarily remain as an element in any civilised consciousness.

CARLYLE: A WRITER OF STRONG OPINIONS AND VOLUMINOUS PROSE

We must begin with Carlyle, the sage of Chelsea who never ceased to be the obstinate peasant of Ecclefechan [Scotland]. His nature was as tortured and "impossible" as his grotesque prose. With his violently puritan, pleasure-hating nature, akin to that of John Knox,[2] he tried to absorb German romanticism, and even the monstrous transcendentalism of [German romantic poet and novelist] Novalis. He longed to be what he was utterly incapable of being, a man of action. . . .

---

1. Arnold attended the prestigious Rugby Prep School and Oxford University.   2. founder of Scottish Presbyterianism

His hatreds were many and manifest, it is hard to discover his loves. He believed that nothing could prosper which was not founded upon what he called veracity, the will of nature, or the commands of God: but everything that he personally disliked was what he meant by unveracious, or contrary to the will of God—Parliaments, Popery, Progress—and if he maintained that men were Godlike individuals, he also asserted that they were mostly fools. His ideas usually came out in a fury of sound which makes him nearly unreadable; his strange concatenations of words and phrases, his jibes and jeers and capital letters, his Germanic constructions, his smokiness, his thunderousness (with its occasional lightning flashes), make it intolerable to read him. "Clotted nonsense"? Clotted, yes, but by no means nonsense. "A sort of Babylonish dialect . . . at times a sort of singular felicity of expression": the contemporary criticisms of *Sartor Resartus* still hold. At first the tremendous nervous vigour appeals; for a few paragraphs one feels an accession of strength: but soon the effect is numbing; it is like the mad rantings of Nathaniel Lee.[3] The storm goes on raging, but one ceases to take any notice.

Yet with all his vociferations Carlyle was an artist. It is not only that he occasionally struck out a memorable phrase, but that he could create a vision of the past. He is not, we are told, to be trusted as a historian, for though he went through enormous travail in seeking out original documents, he distorted history to suit his own arguments. No doubt every historian necessarily does this to some extent; but Carlyle seems to have made no attempt to guard against it; the lower veracity must make way for the higher. For him history was a moral weapon with which to bludgeon his opponents. . . .

And if he was wrong-headed and perverse in a dozen ways, in one respect, in his greatest hatred and contempt, he was right. He loathed Mammon[4] and his works with all his heart. He hated orthodox economics, "the dismal science" with its "inexorable laws", its *laisser faire*, its reduction of men to hopeless slavery. He could not analyse what the horror and the blasphemy were due to, and laid the charge to the door of democracy ("physical-force Chartism"[5] seems to have inspired him with a terror which never left him), but

3. seventeenth-century playwright who lost his reason and was confined in Bedlam, a mental institution   4. from the New Testament; a false god personifying riches, avarice, and worldly gain   5. a movement by workingmen to attain suffrage

he knew in his deepest part that the whole thing was fundamentally wrong.

RUSKIN ON ART AND ECONOMICS

And it was in this realm that Ruskin became his disciple, a disciple who surpassed him in clear-headedness, and had a far more balanced sense of values. Ruskin never believed, as Carlyle did, that the only happiness lay in nerve-racking, back-breaking toil. He was far too sensible to accept the view that work was the sole aim of man's existence on earth: some time at least should be given to the contemplation of God's handiwork, and the enjoyment of beautiful things. He hated industrialism at least as much for creating the Black

---

CARLYLE UNLEASHES HIS STYLE AGAINST INDUSTRIALISTS

In an excerpt from Past and Present, *written in his charged style, Thomas Carlyle chides the leaders of industry to fight against chaos and evil, to lead in the cause of goodness, and to search within themselves for inspiration to save England.*

Captains of Industry are the true Fighters, henceforth recognizable as the only true ones: Fighters against Chaos, Necessity and the Devils and Jötuns;[1] and lead on Mankind in that great, and alone true, and universal warfare; the stars in their courses fighting for them, and all Heaven and all Earth saying audibly, Well done! Let the Captains of Industry retire into their own hearts, and ask solemnly, If there is nothing but vulturous hunger for fine wines, valet reputation and gilt carriages, discoverable there? Of hearts made by the Almighty God I will not believe such a thing. . . . Forgotten as under foulest fat Lethe[2] mud and weeds, there is yet, in all hearts born into this God's-World, a spark of the Godlike slumbering. Awake, O nightmare sleepers; awake, arise, or be for ever fallen! This is not playhouse poetry; it is sober fact. Our England, our world cannot live as it is. It will connect itself with a God again, or go down with nameless throes and fire-consummation to the Devils. Thou who feelest aught of such a Godlike stirring in thee, any faintest intimation of it as through heavy-laden dreams, follow *it*, I conjure thee. Arise, save thyself, be one of those that save thy country.

1. giants of Norse mythology   2. Lethe is the mythological river of forgetfulness.

Thomas Carlyle, *Past and Present*, 1843.

Country as for starving people by the operation of "over-production". . . . His earlier works were devoted to art, to the attempt to make people see things. . . . What was most important, however, was his insistence that art is necessary, that it matters extremely, and that a nation neglects it at its peril. In details he may have been absurd, and often was, but in essentials he was right.

Himself something of an artist—a delicate draughtsman and to some extent a poet—he turned from art to economics. He felt that the landscape and the society brought about by industrialism, and supported by orthodox economics (too often the apologist for the *status quo*), was mortally inimical to art, which could not exist without human life having some decency, some idea other than that of Mammon. It was Carlyle who first convinced him of the horror of industrial economics, and he acknowledged him handsomely as his teacher. But he was more acute than Carlyle: he learnt that ranting and raving was no good; he saw that dictators were no good. . . .

His prose is rarely beautiful for its own sake . . . ; it is a little too drawn out, always a trifle school-ma'amish: but it became in the end a lucid instrument. His incursion into economics caused an uproar. *Unto This Last* began to appear in *The Cornhill Magazine* in 1860 under [William Makepeace] Thackeray's editorship: but the essays "were reprobated in a violent manner", and he was not allowed to continue them. The same happened with *Munera Pulveris*, the mere outline of a work, which began to appear in *Frazer's Magazine*, and was promptly quashed. In details he may have been absurd (his road-making adventures with Oxford under-graduates certainly were), but in essentials he was right. His proposals were "lunatic", but many of them have achieved the stamp of sanity between the sober covers of the statute-book, and it is possible that even his more thorough-going principles may some day be adopted.

ARNOLD: MOVING FORWARD WITH SWEETNESS AND LIGHT

Unlike Carlyle and Ruskin, Matthew Arnold made no plea for a return to the Middle or any other Ages. He did, it is true, write the stimulating if ill-informed *On the Study of Celtic Literature*, rather, one feels, because many people around him were interested in such things than because he himself was attracted towards them. He disliked his own age as much, possibly, as the bearded prophets did, but his remedy was not "go back". For him the cure was to go forward, and the way to do this was not to stir up religious feelings which he himself did not share, but to throw open the doors to the "sweetness and light"[6] of the reason. . . . His range of interests was unusually wide, as a surprised public discovered when the first series of *Essays in Criticism* was published, and though for us to-day his examples are not very well chosen, . . . it is the two series of these criticisms that still remain the important things. The titles of his books, *Culture and Anarchy, Literature and Dogma,* in themselves indicate his trend towards a new humanism, which to a large extent he succeeded in founding as an island of refuge in the religious *débâcle* which took place in the last half of the century. He has been much blamed for his incursions into theology, and for the levity of his tone when dealing with religion, but it is scarcely fair to take this sort of exception. If theology is not the preserve of a clique, if it really is important to every intelligent and cultured man, then surely an intelligent and cultured man has a right to give his views about it. "Levity" is an attitude of mind allowable to a man who wishes to attack something he feels to be dangerous; it is a more effective weapon than solemnity. It was only natural that an unbelieving, but temperamentally religious humanist should anger the believers of his age, as he appears to irritate the believers of this. These, naturally, cannot approve of a man who describes religion as "morality touched by emotion", who defines God as "a stream of tendency, not ourselves, that makes for righteousness"; these definitions do not correspond with their experience. But they did, and do, correspond with the experience of thousands of other people who are ready with him . . . to adore "the sweet reasonableness of Christ". Carlyle appeared more tremendous to his contemporaries; it was Arnold who had the most effect. . . .

England was—and here he borrowed his sharpest arrow from [German writer Heinrich] Heine—Philistine.[7] He battled continuously against provincialism, smugness, narrowness of view, and continually criticised the "Thyestian banquet[8] of claptrap" which, as he saw it, constituted English

---

6. The phrase came originally from Swift's *Battle of the Books.* For him sweetness and light were the qualities that distinguished "the ancients".   7. an attitude of indifference or antagonism toward artistic and cultural values thought to be held by smug, ignorant, middle-class persons   8. at which, Thyestes unwittingly ate the flesh of his two sons

public life. It was essential to see life clearly and to see it whole. Basing his style on French prose, of which he never caught the subtle music (just as he was deaf to French poetry), he was always lucid and sometimes incisive; but towards the end he developed a mannerism of repetition; a sense of fatigue dimly pervades his later writings. As a publicist he is no longer of direct importance, but he permanently affected the thought of this country [England]: much of what is best in our present-day attitude is traceable to Arnold, chiefly in an insistence upon values which are neither materialistic nor religious. His literary criticism still endures. He said much that can be combated; his own favourite phrases, by dint of being repeated by himself and others, have come to seem silly: but his approach was the right approach. He insisted that literature was something important, and that it must finally be judged by a quality of utterance peculiar to itself. That is a commonplace now, but was not so in his own day. It is difficult for those who now deride Arnold to realise how much they owe him on several grounds.

MORRIS: A GREAT MAN

There remains Morris, in some way the greatest, the fullest, the most complete of the Victorians. We may now dislike his wallpaper and his furnishings, tire of his printing, and resent the affected prose of some of his romances; but the vibrations of his tremendous vitality are still felt. He was not a great anything—painter, poet, romancer, or philosopher—but he was a very great man. As a prose-writer he has two distinct sides; the one as a creative writer, which no longer appeals to us; the other in his socialistic work where he was, in the end, far more creative. The pseudomedieval style of his romances is intolerable; but there is this to be said for Morris's medieval stigmata—he really felt and understood certain sides of the Middle Ages. He did not use them as a bludgeon to beat his enemies with, as Carlyle did; he did not flee to them as an escape, after the manner of Ruskin; they were more to him than picturesque material, and in a sense he lived them. But the prose makes it seem as though this love had been an affectation, which it was not. . . .

But *A Dream of John Ball* and the Utopian *News from Nowhere* are written with a keen eye on actuality, and in that clear, decisive, unmannered prose which a sense of actuality brings. Like the three men already discussed, Morris hated the smutching of beauty and the degradation of the individual which was the price paid for commercial supremacy. Once he had become aware of the process he never ceased to battle against "that ocean of half-conscious hypocrisy which is called cultivated society"; and being acute enough to see that the hypocrisy was only half conscious, he realised that the teachings of his predecessors did not cut deep enough. It was no use treating the symptoms; you had to attack the cause, which was not only the economic structure, but the whole framework of society.

CHAPTER 2

The Character of Victorian Writing

The Antiliterary Tone of Victorian Prose

Geoffrey Tillotson

Geoffrey Tillotson explains that Victorian writers rejected literary display and chose to communicate with readers by "speaking" to them through various techniques: author asides, exclamations, didactic prose. In order to convey the earnestness of their agendas to the reader, most writers wrote in a strident tone that tended to remove aesthetic distance. Geoffrey Tillotson taught English language and literature at Berkbeck College, University of London. He is the author of *Criticism and the Nineteenth Century.*

To satisfy the times writers avoided as much as possible what might look studied and 'literary' in the bad sense. For that reason [poet Gerard Manley] Hopkins rejected archaisms almost totally—their use, at least noticeably, 'destroys earnest'. The use of dialect in poems and novels was a way of flourishing the good news that the appearance of sophistication had been avoided. . . .

[Matthew] Arnold as a young man meditating poetry saw how differently a poet should now proceed even from [John] Keats's way:

> And had Shakespeare and [John] Milton lived in the atmosphere of modern feeling, had they had the multitude of new thoughts and feelings to deal with a modern has, I think it likely the style of each would have been far less *curious* and exquisite. For in a *man* style is the saying in the best way *what you have to say.* The *what you have to say* depends on your age. In the 17th century it was a *smaller harvest than now,* and sooner to be reaped: and therefore to its reaper was left time to show it more finely and more curiously. Still more was this the case in the ancient world. The poet's matter being *the hitherto experience of the world, and his own,* increases with every century.

As we should expect, [Thomas] Carlyle grasped the nettle

Reprinted from Geoffrey Tillotson, *A View of Victorian Literature* (Oxford: Clarendon Press, 1978). Reprinted by permission of the Estate of the author.

firmly, his practice corroborating his claim that if a writer has achieved a meaning that is 'genuine', 'deep', and 'noble', most of the expression will have been achieved with it: 'the proper form for embodying [the meaning], the form best suited to the subject and the author will gather round it almost of its own accord'. Even though much is to be read into that 'almost', his advice freed the writer, and especially the poet, from seeing form as existing in the abstract. . . .

Even the slovenliness that [editor Walter] Bagehot thought inevitable in writings designed for the periodicals was preferable to a too visible art. In the *North American Review* for 1853 [poet Arthur] Clough noted that 'poems after classical models, poems from Oriental sources, and the like, have undoubtedly a great literary value. Yet there is no question, it is plain and patent enough, that people much prefer Vanity Fair and Bleak House'.[1] So much for so-called 'literary value'. . . .

The cult of poetry that is 'difficult' or made to look so was also in accordance with this avoidance of seeming to write without earnestness—the difficult poetry of [Robert] Browning, the [poets called the] Spasmodics, Hopkins, and [George] Meredith carried the welcome marks of application. Browning in his 'difficult' poetry took the other course of admitting patches of careless expression that suggested the haste of the runner who bears a message. Clough had mentioned novels. Many of them were trivial and foolish, but the rest, of which he gave two supreme examples, were, as [David] Masson recognized in that same review of another couple of masterpieces, what the earnest age was looking for:

> The manner in which both Thackeray and Dickens people their canvass, the cloud of persons who are watching the action of the story, touching it at detached points, or merely subjected to the observation of the actors, and the way in which that cloud resolves itself into touches, each quivering with its own distinctive individual life, characterize very peculiarly the genius of both authors. It is this wonderful affluence of creative powers which will give them a place in the motley history of modern imaginative literature above that of many producers of more complete works of art [he has been inveighing against periodical publication as making for piecemeal writing that achieved no final unity]. [They show] how plainly their works bear the marks of an unquiet and chaotic time. . . .

---

1. *Vanity Fair* is a novel by William Makepeace Thackeray; *Bleak House* is a novel by Charles Dickens.

Prose ran least risk of looking 'literary', especially prose
published in the reviews. Carlyle made his opinions brilliantly clear in his life of [John] Sterling, reproducing a letter of his of the late thirties:

> Why *sing* your bits of thoughts, if you *can* contrive to speak
> them? By your thought, not by your mode of delivering it, you
> must live or die. . . . And the Age itself, does it not, beyond
> most ages, demand and require clear speech; an Age inca-
> pable of being sung to, in any but a trivial manner, till these
> convulsive agonies and wild revolutionary overturnings
> readjust themselves? Intelligible word of command, not mu-
> sical psalmody and fiddling, is possible in this fell storm of
> battle. Beyond all ages, our Age admonishes whatsoever
> thinking or writing man it has: O, speak to me some wise in-
> telligible speech; your wise meaning in the shortest and
> clearest way; behold I am dying for want of wise meaning,
> and insight into the devouring fact: speak, if you have any
> wisdom! As to song so-called, and your fiddling talent,—even
> if you have one, much more if you have none,—we will talk
> of that a couple of centuries hence, when things are calmer
> again. Homer shall be thrice welcome; but only when Troy is
> *taken*: alas, while the siege lasts, and battle's fury rages every-
> where, what can I do with the Homer? I want Achilles and
> Odysseus,[2] and am enraged to see them trying to be Homers!

In accordance with this view, Arnold, late in the fifties, like
[John] Ruskin before him, veered from verse to prose in an
attempt to gain the ear of the times, as Carlyle had gained it.
Metre, however much it tries to free itself from the smell of
effort and midnight oil, had come to seem inappropriate;
Arnold's free verse, which he imported from Germany, was
designed to ingratiate itself by seeming half-way to prose. . . .

But it was for prose writers that 'speaking' shook off most
of its metaphor. For they often tried to remove the aesthetic
distance between the page and its reader, and became present to him as a physical voice. Authors leaned out of their
books in earnest monologue or would-be dialogue. At the
end of his *Essay on Development*, cutting off the text with
rows of dots, [John Henry] Newman added his pleading personal postscript. In 'Jesuitism' Carlyle gives us a characteristically physical paragraph:

> Prim friend with the black serge gown, with the rosary,
> scapulary, and I know not what other spiritual block-and-
> tackle,—scowl not on me. If in thy poor heart, under its
> rosaries, there dwell any human piety, awestruck reverence
> towards the Supreme Maker, devout compassion towards this

---

2. Achilles is the hero of Homer's *Iliad;* Odysseus of the *Odyssey.*

poor Earth and her sons,—scowl not anathema on me, listen to me; for I swear thou art my brother, in spite of rosaries and scapularies; and recognise thee, though thou canst not me; and with love and pity know thee for a brother, though enchanted into the condition of a spiritual mummy. Hapless creature, curse me not; listen to me, and consider;—perhaps even thou wilt escape from mummyhood, and become once more a living soul!

'Listen to me'—that form of words had also been used by Newman in an early sermon. Thackeray, who cultivated the art of man-to-man commentary, will pause to ask the reader to 'Lay down this book, and think', and Mrs. [Elizabeth] Gaskell, who is dove and eagle by turns, can cry in *Mary Barton:* 'Oh! Orestes![5] you would have made a very tolerable Christian of the nineteenth century!'. . .

EMPHASIS THROUGH TYPEFACE

Queen Victoria, who, after her fashion, exemplified the earnestness of the age, used underlining furiously as correspondent and diarist. In published writings the armoury of the printing-house was called in. Abnormal type and type in abnormal sizes were resorted to. Ruskin used 'bold' type and even, in later editions, sporadic red type. . . . Much italic bespatters verse as well as prose, and Carlyle went further, and italicized a word in part. Carlyle, [Edward Robert] Bulwer Lytton, [Benjamin] Disraeli, Dickens, and Charlotte Brontë emphasized words by the trick of initial capitals. Sometimes phrases or whole sentences received the emphasis of being printed in capitals. . . .

The published voice of the earnest mid-century is sometimes strident. Even Newman's could come near stridency. He cynically remarked in reply to critics that if he had written calmly in his contest with [Charles] Kingsley no one would have believed he was in earnest. On a much earlier occasion he had said: 'The age is so very sluggish, that it will not hear you unless you bawl—you must first tread on its toes, and then apologise.' Carlyle originated this stridency. His first writings—for the *Edinburgh Review*—were almost indistinguishable in point of staid tone from those that surrounded them (no doubt that is why they were acceptable from a novice), but for *Sartor Resartus* he adopted a percus-

---

3. In Greek mythology Orestes was the son of Agamemnon and Clytemnestra, who avenged the murder of his father by killing his mother and her lover.

sive tone deliberately, his aim being to win attention, which he successfully did after the lapse of a decade. Dickens, Ruskin, Charlotte Brontë, Kingsley, [William] Reade, even [Anthony] Trollope and Henry Kingsley, take up his tone, and there is much of it in Hopkins's verse. . . .

It might be expected that such earnestness would choose the medium of formal satire; but this fell into disuse, at least with writers of standing—partly from doubts of the right of one man to condemn another at a time when moral and intellectual canons were generally questioned, and partly from the feelings that satire is too 'literary' a form to be taken seriously: towards the end of his political series *Who's to Blame?*, published during the Crimean War, Newman pronounces the caution, 'Let no man call this satire, for it is most seriously said'. There was also some mistrust of allegory, and of irony when sustained throughout an argument or fiction; the one masterpiece is *The Fair Haven* (1873), Samuel Butler's pretended defence of miracles, with a constructional ingenuity worthy of [satirist Jonathan] Swift.

But humbler forms were promoted, notably the ballad. [William] Wordsworth had seen what strength of thinking it could carry, and passed the knowledge on to [Alfred] Tennyson, Kingsley, and Matthew Arnold. And comic ballads and parodies (the most favoured form of 'imitation') were often topical and hard-hitting, an effective kind of journalism.

Other humble forms were those that carried controversy. Arnold spoke of the 'controversial life we all lead'. Pamphlet and controversial letter to the Press brought the great and lesser writers to the condition of fighters, which condition both Carlyle and Newman saw as proper to man. Newman quoted [Roman satirist] Juvenal's 'Facit indignatio versus',[4] adding: 'I do not feel this in the case of verse; I do, in the case of prose'.

The plainest writing for the times was in such forms. Earnest writers sent letters to newspapers—a collection of them would impress like a bonfire with fireworks. The parson in [Charles] Reade's *It is Never Too Late to Mend* threatens to go over the heads of the Civil Service and write both to the Press and the Queen—'That Lady has a character; one of its strong, unmistakeable feature is a real, tender, active humanity.' Poems could be 'effective . . . engines' even if

4. Indignation will produce verses

'*quasi*-political', but Thackeray (and others) could be wholly and directly political. . . .

The most lasting products of this need to strike hard and produce political results are those achieved by novelists. Novels had been used for practical ends in the late eighteenth century—Mrs. [Elizabeth] Inchbald's *Simple Story*, [William] Godwin's *Caleb Williams*, [Robert] Bage's *Hermsprong* all belong to the 1790s. When defending the novel form Jane Austen had claimed it as the repository of the highest powers of a writer, powers that in earlier times had produced epics and tragedies. Half a century later, in *Bentley's Quarterly Review* for 1859, [critic] Anne Mozley concentrated on a novel's effect on its reader. While being 'amused' by it, as all novel readers insist on being, not only do 'we expect to have our feelings roused, our taste cultivated', but also, in these bad days, 'our social conscience refined and quickened'. And she adds: 'To these requirements, even to the last, all must subscribe'. By that time there had been many novels that hoped to refine and quicken a reader's conscience. In 1850 a reviewer could note that 'books of fiction are all now connected in some way with the condition of society', and six years later a letter to *The Times* from Sidney Godolphin Osborne, the well-known clergyman and philanthropist, noted (in the course of his argument for the reinstating of Sunday band-playing in the Parks) that not only the philanthropists but the novelists 'have left no one feature of [the] condition [of the 'working-classes in our great towns'] unmasked'. It is not the concern of a critic and even a historian of literature to recount the fortunes of literature in producing a practical effect on the life of the time, though it is amusing to recall that *Nicholas Nickleby* led to a closing-down and bankruptcy of schools in Yorkshire, and that after the emergence of Bumble in the course of the serial publication of *Oliver Twist* there were lectures in Chelsea rebutting the implied charges against parochial maladministration. To Dickens's credit, one must pause to modify the widely held view that as a novelist-reformer he was often beating at an open door. Fitzjames Stephen described him as 'get[ting] his first notions of an abuse from the discussions that accompany its removal', a view later supported by [critic] Humphry House. It was unlikely that anybody in that widely earnest age could claim to be the first mover towards a particular reform, and Dickens no doubt usually joined his earnest and far-carrying voice to that of others.

Victorian Novels Have a Moral Design

John R. Reed

John R. Reed argues that realism is blended with
moral idealism in Victorian literature but that teaching readers to choose good over evil supersedes the
presentation of realistic characters and stories. For
many writers, suffering and illness provide suitable
conventions to humble the proud and tame the wild.
However, according to Reed, by the end of the nineteenth century this serious moral purpose no longer
seemed suitable to an age that was becoming more
materialistic. John R. Reed has taught English at
Wayne State University in Detroit, Michigan. He is
the author of *Perception and Design in Tennyson's*
Idylles of the King and *English Literature in Transition: 1880–1920.*

In order to read the literature of the Victorian period accu-
rately and rewardingly, it is necessary to acknowledge and
recover the forms of stylization and convention with which
Victorian authors and audiences were familiar.

Victorian literature was not realistic in the same sense as
that attributed to contemporary literature. In some ways it
had as much in common with medieval literature as with
twentieth-century writing, for behind much of Victorian literature were the now-explicit, now-implied conventional
patterns and stylized characters or scenes that endowed it
with a dimension which, accepted by readers of that time,
are no longer immediately evident to modern readers; in
most cases, those patterns and stylizations were moral. For
us, circumstantial authenticity is a conclusive test of realism, but for Victorian writers, fidelity to moral ideas was
also important. . . .

The rendering of the world as one sees it is subordinate to

Excerpted from John R. Reed, *Victorian Conventions* (Athens: Ohio University Press,
1975). Copyright ©1975 by John R. Reed. Reprinted by permission of the author.

the greater purpose of superintending readers' perceptions of good and evil, and counselling the proper preference. R.L. Stevenson, attempting to resolve the quarrel between realists and idealists, said that realism involved the technical method, not the truth of a work of art. By the end of the century, it is true, some felt that the distinction was a false one. As Basil Hallward says in Oscar Wilde's *The Picture of Dorian Gray* (1890), "We in our madness have separated the two [body and soul] and have invented a realism that is vulgar, and an ideality that is void." But throughout the century, there was a continuing belief that the ideal was achievable through the real. . . .

In Victorian literature, what we would call realistic motivation is often incorporate with type fulfillment. Characters do not act according to a system of humors or ruling passions, nor are they moved by the complexes and neuroses of the twentieth-century man; instead, they exhibit predictable combinations of attributes which result in conventional types. These types, moreover, often operate within equally conventional moral designs. In this way, Victorian writers could be faithful to the things of this world while employing a highly emblematic and occasionally symbolic manner of writing that modern criticism, for some obscure reason, tends to consider incompatible with their circumstantial realism. . . .

The discovery of a superior morality in the doings of secular men is, after all, the object of much Victorian literature. Indications of belief in a universal design might vary considerably from one writer to the next. For [Alfred] Tennyson, all of existence might seem to be a "toil coöperant to an end," while later, less hopeful writers might view experience as a game played by vague Immortals or Indefinable Powers, as [Thomas] Hardy described them at different times. Nonetheless, throughout Victorian literature there runs a tradition of an assumed design of which individual lives are but a part. Realism, the faithful depiction of the details of life, therefore becomes compatible with idealism, which assumes a larger scheme to which those details are subordinate. . . .

A MORAL STRUCTURE UNDERLIES VICTORIAN LITERATURE

The English may or may not have been, in the years of their international supremacy, a sentimental race inclined to view existence as a moral romance, but in their literature of the nineteenth century the tendency to conceive of existence in terms of moral structures with foundations of fairy-tale morality is evident. . . .

Anthony Trollope averred [in his *Autobiography*] that "the novelist, if he have a conscience, must preach his sermon with the same purpose as the clergyman, and must have his own system of ethics." Moreover, for Trollope, as for many another Victorian writer, it was the "system of ethics," not the narrative action, that determined the form of the novel. Explaining that incidents and personages of his novel, *Phineas Finn*, developed as they were written, Trollope adds, "But the evil and good of my puppets, and how the evil would always lead to evil, and the good produce good,—that was clear to me as the stars on a summer night.". . .

Writers of the stature of [Charles] Dickens did not hesitate to defend their moral arguments. And even in autobiography, as in [George] Borrow's unlikely accounts, readers would not have been offended, presumably, to have learned that certain facts had been altered to fit the more important moral structure of the accounts. . . .

Elsewhere, I have stated the principal moral design operating in Tennyson's poetry. It is a design familiar to poets, novelists, historians, and social commentators alike. The movement is from an uninformed and sometimes pleasing condition, through redemptive struggle and suffering, to joy or resignation. For Tennyson, the movement was generally from pride, to suffering and humility, to redemption in selflessness. There are, however, other variations of the general scheme. This pervasive literary design applied not only to the individual, but could be historical, or, more significantly, metaphysical. . . .

SUFFERING IS SIGNIFICANT IN VICTORIAN LITERATURE

Victorian readers, accustomed to consider earthly existence as probation for eternity, did not find affirmations of the redemptive effects of suffering unusual in their literature. However, even without the prospect of eternity, suffering retained its therapeutic associations for a surprising number of writers and moralists largely because it acquired an esthetic and secular importance.

George Alfred Lawrence's *Guy Livingstone, or "Thorough"* (1857) commends [Charlotte Yonge's] *The Heir of Redclyffe* (1853) and [William Makepeace Thackeray's] *The Newcomes* (1853–54) for their superb treatment of "simple and quiet sorrows." But these novels have more than "simple and quiet sorrows" in common in that they utilize the moral design that I have already described. In Thackeray's novel, several characters follow the necessary route from pride, through humility, to redemptive selflessness. Young Lord Kew's involvement in a duel is considered a punishment for an earlier life of "prodigality." Kew is wounded, but his injury occasions a salubrious illness which leads to reform by forcing him to make up "his account of the vain life" he has led. Kew's is a simple and sharply defined case. More subtly, Clive Newcome also moves from the pride of youth and love, through imprudence and idleness, to his necessary humbling, which consequently provides its reward. And even the excellent Colonel, Clive's father, moves from staunch pride in his goodness, to a selfless imprudence, which is corrected by a thorough humbling. Colonel Newcome's withdrawal to the Grey Friars almshouse is the outstanding example of worthwhile humility in the novel, concluding with an undeniable sign of salvation in the Colonel's dying answer of "Ad Sum"[1] to the last heavenly call.

Ethel Newcome's case is more representative. She is beautiful and haughty, and her principal sins are vanity and pride, but "In after life, care and thought subdued her pride, and she learned to look at society more good naturedly." Ethel's sufferings come through family scandal and Clive's marriage to the innocent Rosa Mackenzie, who fails to make Clive genuinely happy. Humiliated by the prospect of a loveless marriage, Ethel's conscience revives, and thereafter vanity yields to humility. "She is very much changed since you knew her," Pendennis says to Colonel Newcome; "Very much changed and very much improved." Pendennis himself has been alerted to Ethel's transformation by his own faultless wife, who now sees the good in the once vain beauty. "Who would have thought this was the girl of your glaring London ballroom? If she has had grief to bear, how it has chastened and improved her." Ethel devotes herself to good works and assistance to the poor; she no longer resembles Judith, Salome, and Diana,[2] but assumes a saint-like aspect and is likened to the Good Samaritan.[3] Accord-

---

1. "I'm Here" 2. In the Old Testament, Judith is a Jewish heroine who rescued her people by slaying an Assyrian general. In the New Testament, Salome is niece of Harod, who granted her the head of John the Baptist in return for her dancing. In Roman mythology, Diana is the virgin goddess of the hunt. 3. in the New Testament parable, the passerby who is the only person to aid a man who had been beaten and robbed

ingly, Ethel is rewarded by her union with Clive, which is implied at the novel's conclusion. . . .

ILLNESS LEADS TO REDEMPTION

Guy Livingstone is one of the most conventional of nineteenth-century novels in that it employs a large number of literary conventions. Moreover, because of its popularity, it contributed to the solidifying of those conventions. Its titular hero, a proud, passionate, and physically imposing man, became so well known that Matthew Arnold, in his essay on [Russian novelist Leo] Tolstoy, referred confidently to "the Guy Livingstone type." This gifted, but self-indulgent hero falls in love with the virtuous Constance Brandon, while failing to reject altogether the fascinations of Flora Bellasys. As a result of momentary intoxication with the seductive Flora, Guy loses Constance, who gradually fails in health, until, on her deathbed, she calls her guilty lover to her. Though he has given himself up to dissipation, the vision of his saintly love, whose death is a "victory" of "loyalty and right," brings him back to his senses, and he promises to change his ways. . . .

"The Valley of the Shadow of Death" is the title of a chapter in Charlotte Brontë's *Shirley* (1849), which describes Caroline Helstone's illness, caused by her unsatisfied craving for love. Caroline does not die, but learns through her illness to harness passions to moral purpose and is therefore prepared to attend Robert Moore in his subsequent illness and to recommend the lesson of her own suffering as a model. Accordingly, when Robert recovers, he is no longer the "proud angry, disappointed man" that he had been, and he and Caroline marry. The quasi-illnesses of Louis and Shirley mirror Robert and Caroline's genuine movement through the valley of the shadow of death. In each case, passion is subdued and pride overcome. Each illness, no matter how slight, serves as a moral bloodletting that braces the spirit. The pattern is absolutely formulaic in Anne Thackeray Ritchie's *The Story of Elizabeth* (1867), where Elizabeth Gilmore falls ill from frustrated love, and is tended by Miss Dampier, a splendid moral model. Elizabeth recovers as the birds stir in the spring to their busy life. "Elizabeth's life too, began anew from this hour." Devoting herself to charitable activity, Elizabeth is rewarded by the return of her first love and marriage. . . .

Dickens employed the convention frequently in his novels.

Martin Chuzzlewit discovers through physical illness and pride's abasement, the utter selfishness of his early life, and acquires the virtues of "humility and steadfastness." Dick Swiveller undergoes a similar experience. Redemptive suffering in *Great Expectations* cleanses Pip of his selfishness and pride, opening for him a life of humility and steadfastness. In *Our Mutual Friend*, Dickens used the moral design in Eugene's salubrious illness and apparently redemptive recovery, but he also treated it ironically in the unredemptive recovery of Rogue Riderhood and the mimic baptism of Wegg in his own dust cart. . . .

Most illnesses in Victorian literature stay close to conventional moral sentiments, and echoes of the Bible, as has already been evident, strengthen the association. In Books 9 and 10 of Miss [Mary] Braddon's *Charlotte's Inheritance* (1868), in which Charlotte Halliday is seriously ill and in danger of dying (as a result of poisoning, as it turns out), section headings give us a strong clue to the importance of the event. Book 9 is entitled "Through the Furnace," and Chapter 1 of Book 10 is called "Out of the Dark Valley." In this instance, however, illness operates on the witness, not the sufferer. When Charlotte recovers, Valentine Hawkeshurst, her lover, is relieved: "He had reason to rejoice; for he had passed through the valley of the shadow of death." He has faced the darkness, not of his own, but of Charlotte's possible death; now he ascends into the light with his beloved: "The struggle had been dire, the agony of suspense a supreme torture; but from the awful contest the man came forth a better and a wiser man. Whatever strength of principle had been wanting to complete the work of reformation inaugurated by love, had been gained by Valentine Hawkeshurst during the period of Charlotte's illness.". . .

Often recovery from illness is associated with natural settings of revival and rebirth in Victorian literature, but in [George Meredith's] *The Adventures of Harry Richmond* (1871) it is the rebellion of natural forces—in the form of a gypsy attack—that brings on Harry's malady. This in turn cures him of his fanciful dreams and teaches him to focus upon more approachable goals, as in his decision to choose his proper mate, not from the aristocracy, but from his own rank. Neville Beauchamp, in [George Meredith's] *Beauchamp's Career* (1876), has a similar awakening after illness; declaring "I wake from illness with my eyes open," he realizes that the true object of his affections should be, not the cultivated and wealthy Cecilia Halkett, but the simpler Jenny, the more suitable mate for his reforming intentions. Diana Warwick, in [George Meredith's] *Diana of the Crossways* (1885), lapses into a mild illness after a disappointment in love, and Meredith, describing how her resort to nature revives her, remarks, "Her fall had brought her renovatingly to earth, and the saving naturalness of the woman recreated her childlike."

There was nothing uncommon in the Victorian utilization of illness, but during the nineteenth century it acquired a moral function not always associated with physical suffering, and the moral associations continued into the twentieth century so that so notable a writer as [German novelist] Thomas Mann could reassert the proposition, assumed so generally in Victorian literature, that "one must go through the deep experience of sickness and death to arrive at a higher sanity and health; in just the same way that one must have a knowledge of sin in order to find redemption.". . .

THE CONVENTIONAL MORAL STRUCTURE CHANGED

Not all writers and their readers would have agreed that suffering was necessarily a moral good. Wilkie Collins declared in *Armadale* that "Suffering can, and does, develop the latent evil that there is in humanity, as well as the latent good." And Miss Wade in *Little Dorrit* exhibits this sentiment in Dickens' novel, as do the suffering multitudes in *Barnaby Rudge* and *A Tale of Two Cities*. By 1884, [George] Gissing could picture unfavorably the belief that life was meant to be a test and an ordeal in the fanatical Mrs. Bygrave in *The Unclassed*. Nor were those who wished to maintain a moral stability while refashioning man's mode of perceiving existence likely to agree with simple attitudes concerning the sanctification of suffering and renunciation. . . .

It became more and more difficult for a culture deeply committed to material progress and comforts to excuse or explain pain. For some the justification itself became a weak consolation of an ambiguous evolution, expressed by H.G. Wells in *The Time Machine* in the epigrammatic phrase: "We are kept keen on the grindstone of pain and necessity. . . ." From cleansing, redemptive fires to grim mechanical grindstones is a sad course, and yet the progress of metaphors indicates a genuine movement of thought in the age. The ecstatic imagery of flame argued an energy and passion equated with the natural exuberance of existence, while the passage through the Valley of the Shadow of Death, drawn from Scripture, captured the vitality of a genuine movement in space and time, through darkness to light. The man-made grindstone, on the other hand, implies nothing more than a fierce but passionless movement strictly confined in space, with one tedious and doubtful effect.

Early Victorian sentiments had assumed a human will driven by passions that must be restrained to harmonize with the divine plan like a supreme music. By the end of the century, the relentless wheel of circumstance and chance seemed to deprive man of the volition that made his part in a larger plan credible. If man was not on a journey, where he could take wrong turnings and be singed for them, but on a conveyor belt of history, then the grand moral design was not a model, but a mockery. Acknowledgment of this possibility bred an increased self-consciousness among Victorian writers about the stylizations of their time.

Victorian Writers Catered to an Increasing Readership

Richard D. Altick

Richard D. Altick focuses on the reading habits of working- and middle-class Victorians, calling the working class semiliterates who read thrillers and informative weekly papers. The middle classes, the largest and most diverse reading audience, could afford serial publications of novels and quarterly, monthly, and weekly periodicals. Besides fiction, periodicals published high-quality nonfiction written by philosophers, scientists, and clergymen analyzing the issues of the day and offering educated opinions about them. Many of the best Victorian prose writers first published their works in the periodicals. Richard D. Altick was an English professor at Ohio State University in Columbus. He is the author of several books, including *The Scholar Adventurer, The Art of Literary Research,* and *Victorian Studies in Scarlet.*

Although it is customary to speak of "the reading public"—singular—in connection with the audience for the printed word, in Victorian times that audience, like today's, was not really a cohesive, homogeneous unit but a whole cluster of publics, as various as the society to which they belonged.

The upper class probably read neither more nor less than it had done in earlier centuries, when it had subsidized authors through patronage and some of its members had themselves contributed to the national literature. Walter Bagehot, one of the shrewdest mid-Victorian social commentators, probably was not far from the truth when he remarked, "A great part of the 'best' English people keep their minds in a state of decorous dullness." At all events, the up-

Excerpted from *Victorian People and Ideas: A Companion for the Modern Reader of Victorian Literature*, by Richard D. Altick. Copyright ©1973 by W.W. Norton & Company, Inc. Reprinted by permission of W.W. Norton & Company, Inc.

per ranks formed a negligible fraction of the Victorian reading public.

WORKING-CLASS READERS

Some members of the working class read, but it is impossible to tell, except in the most general way, how numerous they were. The crucial question, naturally, is that of literacy. . . . Popular education during most of the century was spotty and ineffectual, though as the years passed it reached more and more people. The national literacy rate for adults, based on the ability to inscribe one's name in the marriage register, rose from 67 per cent (male) and 51 per cent (female) in 1841 to approximately 97 per cent for both sexes in 1900. But these figures exaggerate the incidence of reading ability among the masses. Many thousands who could trace their names could not read a word of print. Because the figures do not distinguish among social classes, the over-all national rate was pushed upward by the high incidence of literacy in the middle and upper classes, and if it were possible to segregate the working class in these statistics, it would be seen that the literacy rate there was markedly below the national average. More significant figures come from local surveys. In 1833, in an artisan-class district of London, 777 parents could read and 267 could not; in 1845, 75 per cent of the children leaving 176 Midland schools (after an average attendance of a year and a half) were, for all practical purposes, illiterate. Many observers reported that whatever reading skill a child acquired during his brief attendance at school often was irretrievably lost, through insufficient practice while in the classroom or subsequent disuse. In the year the Second Reform Bill was passed (1867), a house-to-house canvass in Manchester revealed that barely more than half the adults could read. . . .

Some intellectually ambitious workers applied themselves to serious books, working their way through them slowly, attentively, and retentively. But the majority chose books and papers written expressly for an audience of semiliterates whose requirements were simple but demanding. Because they possessed virtually no general information, their reading matter had to be devoid of all but the most familiar literary and historical allusions; they could not be expected to waste time puzzling over any more recondite kind. And because their attention spans were short, they needed a running supply of excitements, brief and to the point, and sentences and paragraphs to match.

For these readers were published incalculable quantities of easily digestible books and papers: "penny dreadfuls" and "shilling shockers," the equivalent of the American dime novels of the same epoch; cheap weeklies featuring interminable serializations of thrilling fiction (for men and boys) and sentimental tales (for women and girls); drastic condensations of "standard literature," among them some literary classics such as [Walter] Scott's romances; broadsides reporting sensational news events such as fires, murders, and natural calamities; cheap Sunday newspapers enlivened with radical politics and extensive police reports. The moral gamut ran from religious tracts to semi-pornographic ballads. There was an extensive Victorian literary sub-culture, but, except for the self-taught workmen who, in a way of speaking, read above their station, the lasting works of literature which their age produced seldom filtered down to the semi-literate audience. To us, the interest of the printed matter which they actually devoured is sociological, not literary. The tart phrase a late Victorian prime minister applied specifically to the cheap "instructive and entertaining" miscellaneous weeklies of the *Tit-Bits* type describes most contemporary working-class reading matter: "Written by office boys for office boys."

MIDDLE-CLASS READERS

The audience for the literature which continues to be read today was concentrated, therefore, in the middle class. It was primarily there that printed matter in all its forms became a much more familiar accompaniment to everyday living than ever before, and the activity of reading occupied a notably larger portion of many persons' free time. The same modest affluence which enabled them to hire servants and artisans gave them additional pocket money to lay out for "a good read."

The middle-class market for print was divided into many interest-groups: the young, the religious, the fashionable, the educated, the ambitious, the time-killing. As each of these audiences grew, publishers catered to it by finding writers and forms to meet its peculiar requirements. But there was much overlapping. A few Victorian authors, such as [Charles] Dickens and [Alfred] Tennyson, appealed to almost every sector of the middle-class public and had a following in the more literate reaches of the working class as well.

Many readers, furthermore, had diverse tastes; what they read at a given time depended on their mood and what was being talked about. They read for amusement, to pass the time pleasantly and without intellectual strain. Hence the mounting popularity of fiction, which was usually regarded as entertainment and only gradually, in the course of the era, acquired a measure of critical acceptance as a serious art form. Novels had the same place in many intelligent readers' diet that detective stories and science fiction have had more recently: they relaxed the mind after its strenuous labors. [Essayist Thomas Babington] Macaulay, for example, annually consumed hundreds of worthless novels, the more sentimental or incredible the better. It is a tribute to Victorian taste that some of the best novels of the time sold as well as did many of the worst.

Victorian readers also went in for inspiration. Moralized stories and biographies, sermons, religious literature of all kinds, including periodicals for Sunday reading, gushed from the presses by the ton. They were not always dull reading, by any means. The true-life and fictional narratives, whatever their tincture of moral uplift, were designed to compete with secular reading matter on its own terms, and so they contained plenty of suspense and thrilling episodes. Even the sermons—not the learned variety, but those appropriate to revival meetings and similar evangelical occasions—had some of the qualities of third-rate fiction, not least its fustian[1] style.

The Victorians, finally, read to learn. There was an enormous literature of information, some ponderous and some lightweight, on every topic of human interest, from celestial mechanics to what might be seen under a microscope, from Arctic exploration to pinmaking, from grave social questions to pithy anecdotes. Relative to the total population, there was a much larger audience for serious writing in Victorian times than in ours. Around what would now be called the intelligentsia existed . . . a large periphery of decently educated readers, not in any sense erudite, who devoted themselves in after-business hours to learning more about the world they lived in and its inhabitants. They supported, sometimes

---

1. pretentious; bombastic

handsomely, more "quality" magazines and reviews than our modern culture can accommodate, and made it possible for commercial firms to issue innumerable books of a sort which would now be published, if published at all, by university presses.

THE EFFECTS OF EDUCATION AND PRINTING TECHNOLOGY

That so many people in what were then called "the middling walks of life"—and even, to a degree, the "humbler" ones— were lifelong devotees of books is evidence of a cultural climate which stressed the value of education and ideas, and exalted books as the noblest product and symbol of civilization. To the Victorians, the printing press driven by a steam engine was, indeed, the most pregnant emblem of their achievement and aspirations. Gutenberg[2] was virtually a culture hero, and his invention, it was thought, was the most potent instrument of social improvement ever conceived. . . .

The expansion of the reading public was accompanied— it is impossible to distinguish cause from effect here—by technological advances which made the printed word both cheaper and more readily accessible than it had ever been before. The steam press, the stereotyping process,[3] new papermaking machinery and the adoption of cheaper ingredients than the former staple of rags, machinery for prefabricating bindings, and, late in the century, mechanized typesetting enabled books, magazines, and newspapers to take their place among the other Victorian commodities that were cheapened by mass production and made more widely available by energetic merchandising. By the end of the century English publishing had undergone a revolution. From a sleepy, unimportant trade whose practices differed little from those prevailing in Shakespeare's time it had grown into a bustling business, as inventive, competitive, and specialized as any other branch of Victorian commerce.

In the first half of the century, however, books were something of a luxury item, despite the declining costs of production. Publishers usually sold a substantial part of an edition to commercial circulating libraries at a big discount, meanwhile keeping the retail price artificially high. Many readers therefore got their books, especially newly published ones,

---

2. German printer Johannes Gutenberg is traditionally considered the inventor of movable type in the fifteenth century.   3. making metal frames for raised type

from the libraries, which lent them for an annual subscription. After 1850, as has been noted, free libraries began to appear in various towns and cities throughout the country; these catered to both the middle and working classes.

NUMBER PUBLICATIONS, QUARTERLIES, MONTHLIES, AND WEEKLIES

From the time of *Pickwick Papers* (1836–37) to the sixties, a certain amount of popular fiction, including a dozen of Dickens' own novels, four of [William Makepeace] Thackeray's, and eight of [Anthony] Trollope's, appeared in monthly or weekly installments over periods of up to eighteen months or two years. Publication in numbers or parts, as they were called, brought down the price to the buyer. Each monthly number usually cost a shilling and the total outlay amounted sometimes to only two-thirds the price of a hardbound novel. Like magazine serialization, number publication presented the author with opportunities and technical problems that are usefully borne in mind in any critical analysis of fiction which first appeared in installments. During the middle decades of the century part-issue existed side by side with magazine serialization, but by the seventies it was crowded out by the magazines, which had the advantage of offering the reader, at no increase in price, not only a segment of a novel but a variety of other features. Once in a while new non-fiction was issued in parts. [Thomas] Carlyle's *Latter-Day Pamphlets* came out in eight monthly numbers (1850), and [John Henry] Newman's *Apologia* in seven weekly ones (1864). . . .

This was the great age of English periodicals. In the beginning of the Victorian era, the magisterial quarterly reviews, the Whig *Edinburgh* (founded 1802), its rival the Tory *Quarterly* (1809), and the Benthamite *Westminster* (1824), shared the top intellectual level. Enjoying circulations which, in proportion to the size of the reading public, were much greater than any comparable periodical can boast today, these powerful journals were edited and written by some of the era's leading authors and public men. Most of Macaulay's essays, for example, were written for the *Edinburgh.*

The quarterlies had to share room with the monthly magazines, typified in the first Victorian decades by *Blackwood's Edinburgh Magazine* (1817) and *Fraser's Magazine* (1830). These were distinguished by lively writing, irreverence, and a partisanship which sometimes exceeded that of the opinionated quarterlies. Instead of the lengthy essays posing as book reviews which were the quarterlies' staple, each issue of the monthlies had a variety of contents, short and serialized fiction, topical articles, true narratives, satirical essays. In *Fraser's* first appeared Carlyle's *Sartor Resartus* (as well as many of his separate essays), Thackeray's *Yellowplush Papers*, and [Charles] Kingsley's *Yeast.*

In the forties and fifties the miscellaneous magazines were joined by weekly papers addressed to a wider "family" audience. *Punch* (1841) was among the first and incomparably the greatest of the Victorian humorous journals, printing the work of many talented writers and artists and both reflecting and exerting much influence on middle-class opinion. Its cheaper (non-humorous) contemporaries, such as Dickens' *Household Words* (1850–59) and that paper's successor, *All the Year Round,* were edited for a still larger, less sophisticated readership. In addition to short articles on topics of current interest and chatty essays, these weeklies featured serial fiction—Dickens' *Hard Times* and Mrs. [Elizabeth] Gaskell's *Cranford* in the case of *Household Words,* and *Great Expectations,* Wilkie Collins' pioneer detective stories *The Woman in White* and *The Moonstone,* and three of Trollope's novels in that of *All the Year Round.*

A new generation of monthly magazines and middlebrow reviews in the sixties and seventies continued to refine the formula that was proving so attractive to the better educated portion of the middle-class audience. The spectacularly successful *Cornhill Magazine* (1860) serialized three minor novels by Thackeray, its first editor, as well as George Eliot's *Romola,* Trollope's *Framley Parsonage,* and [Thomas] Hardy's *Far from the Madding Crowd.* In the *Fortnightly Review* (1865) appeared three of Trollope's novels as well as most of [George] Meredith's *Diana of the Crossways* and *The Tragic Comedians.* The leading novelists wrote not only for the quality periodicals but for their numerous weekly and monthly imitators, which were slanted toward a more popular audience. Trollope's novels appeared in ten magazines representing various levels, Hardy's and [Charles] Reade's in almost as many.

HIGH-QUALITY NON-FICTION

But perhaps most interesting to the modern reader who browses in the bound files of the most distinguished periodicals is the amount and excellence of their non-fiction. The novels they serialized leavened a loaf rich in intellectual vitamins. This higher journalism—there is no better term for it—was an art indigenous to the Victorian periodical edited for the intelligent lay reader. Its forte was the treatment of a subject of interest to the educated mind, in a manner that was serious but not heavy, urbane rather than facetious or sedulously "bright." The writers in that genre discovered a happy middle way between vulgarization and pedantry, an art almost lost today because evidently there is no demand for it.

Much Victorian higher journalism was purely expository, but at least a comparable amount was devoted to stating points of view or advocating courses of public action. There was a more than coincidental relationship between the enlargement of the printed medium and the simultaneous development of political democracy. Public opinion became for the first time a decisive influence, an agent of change. . . .

The claim, made in 1832 and again in 1846, that "the people had triumphed"[4] was not mere empty rhetoric. They had, thanks to a press that stirred more men's thinking than had ever been stirred before. It was not surprising, therefore, that faith should grow in the effectiveness of what John Stuart Mill called "the collective will" as the prime influence on decision-making, and that the press should become the chief instrument of its expression.

Although little of this enormous body of printed argument and exhortation has survived as literature, it provided the matrix for the masterpieces of social discussion which are still read today. Few of the great writers on social questions, including the novelists, were affiliated with any individual movement which sought to bring public opinion to bear on Parliament or other centers of power. But their expressions of personal opinion were uttered in a spacious forum resounding to many voices, and the particular nature of their own rhetoric is best defined when it is compared with the persuasive techniques of their workaday contemporaries. A man who, like most educated Victorians, read a fair sample of the barrage of topical argument, year after year, could not avoid having his personal style and strategy affected by it when he joined the symposium.

Alongside this babel of controversial voices—propaganda

4. in mobilizing public opinion to influence passage of the Reform Bills

in the ordinary sense of doctrinaire partisanship—existed a more disinterested kind of discussion whose subject was issues rather than causes. Here the would-be persuaders were ordinarily not zealots but men of controlled intelligence— the philosophers, scientists, government officials, lawyers, clergymen, higher journalists who were the real opinion-makers. They subjected contemporary problems and institutions to a continuous process of analysis and criticism, and they did so in a manner noteworthy for its restraint and civility. However sharply they differed from one another, they wrote like gentlemen. Rant was a method of argumentation associated with working-class radicals and Wesleyan [religious] revivalists; courtesy of discourse was the sign of the well-bred scholar. Perhaps this is one reason why they had an effect reaching far beyond specific decisions in Parliament and governmental policies. Their vigorous but mannerly discussion influenced the long-term direction of public thought and action. Even some printed government documents, indeed, had this quality and effect. John Simon's annual reports as the public health officer, first for the City of London and then for the national government, were praised in the *Times* for their "terse, forcible, and graphic" style, which possessed "real eloquence, intense and fervid, reaching the climax of a deep and almost terrible earnestness." Despite their repulsive subject-matter, their editions were quickly sold out. There seems little question that the literary quality of this kind of "public prose," such a far cry from the customary jargon of bureaucrats, had much to do with awakening the public to the gravity of certain social problems and stirring it to demand—and get—action.

PROSE ENGAGED THE PUBLIC AND PROVIDED A VALVE FOR ENMITIES

Although books and magazines and newspapers echoed with the shibboleths and cant of contemporary economic, political, social, religious, and moral opinion, they could also be the most formidable enemies of smugness. "If," as a leading modern Labour Party intellectual has put it, "millions of people in Victorian Britain were complacent, there were armies of intellectual non-conformists breaking in on that complacency and compelling their countrymen to accept the facts of change and the discoveries of science, ready to court unpopularity by challenging the Victorian bishops and shattering the illusions of the Victorian politicians. . . . Victorian Britain was not a democracy—the working class was still excluded from any real share in government. But it was a free society in which the ideas bubbling out of the controversy of public opinion fashioned and re-fashioned the form of the State. . . .

Carlyle's *Sartor Resartus,* Macaulay's essays extolling the blessings of Whig governance, [John] Ruskin's attacks on political economy and associated evils in *"Unto This Last"* and *Munera Pulveris,* [Matthew] Arnold's *Culture and Anarchy,* [Thomas] Huxley's essays on science and education, [William] Morris' socialistic preachments—all originally appeared in Victorian periodicals and were part of the constant debate which brought differences into the open and engaged the minds and emotions of their readers.

The press had as many voices as it had audiences. Carlyle's thunderings were echoed, at the distance of a generation, by Arnold's suave and malicious irony; and while some spoke to the select few, others addressed the multitude. It was thanks to this versatility, this many-voicedness, that the several classes came to a certain understanding of one another's positions in the fluid state of society. So long as the press kept the crucible of controversy seething, the nation's mind could not stagnate. And because the press provided at the same time a safety valve by which class enmities and other potentially dangerous differences could be vented without harm, Victorian England escaped class struggle. The Victorians had been persuaded that the press was mightier than either pulpit or cannon, and that the health of an ailing society could be restored by the reasonableness of the printed word. Insofar as the nation entered the twentieth century intact and prosperous, its mind vigorous and its freedoms unabridged, that faith was not misplaced.

Victorian Nonfiction Possesses Literary Qualities

John D. Cooke and Lionel Stevenson

John D. Cooke and Lionel Stevenson survey popular nonfiction topics of the Victorian era and the authors who wrote about them—Thomas Carlyle, John Henry Newman, John Stuart Mill, John Ruskin, Matthew Arnold, and Thomas Babington Macaulay. Cooke and Stevenson found among diverse styles and topics that all of these writers wrote with fine literary qualities. Victorian readers responded to this literary style by eagerly reading philosophy, theology, science, travel, social science, and history. John D. Cooke and Lionel Stevenson taught English at the University of Southern California. Cooke is the editor of *Minor Victorian Poets;* Stevenson is the author of *The Life of William Makepeace Thackeray.*

The Victorian age was so strongly excited over opinions, ideas, theories, and even the acquiring of new information, that many books of expository prose attained not only the wide influence but also the qualities of originality and emotional force which put them into the class of literature. Philosophy, religion, physical science, political theory, economics, and history all contributed books which were written with distinguished style and originality.

One trait was shared by practically all of these books: they were long. Accordingly, the modern reader has little opportunity of becoming familiar with them. Sample excerpts are incapable of giving a true impression of the chief writings of [Thomas] Carlyle or [John] Ruskin, [Charles] Darwin or [Herbert] Spencer, [John Stuart] Mill or [Thomas Babington] Macaulay. Writing in a day when fewer competing interests distracted a reader's attention, they assumed that their

Excerpted from John D. Cooke and Lionel Stevenson, *English Literature of the Victorian Period* (New York: Appleton-Century-Crofts, 1949).

subject-matter was important enough to deserve full development. The various main types of expository prose will here be discussed separately, though some authors were equally prominent in more than one category, and sometimes a single book is hard to assign because it ranges from one category into another.

THE VERSATILE AND POSITIVE THOMAS CARLYLE

The oldest of all the Victorians, and the most positive of the many strong personalities that expressed themselves in literature, was Thomas Carlyle. Owing to his slow struggle to gain an education and a start in his literary career, he was publishing his first books alongside men ten or twelve years younger. In his long lifetime he wrote in many of the different fields of prose.

It is impossible to separate Carlyle's writings on "philosophy" from those on economic and social subjects. His various doctrines of work, duty, and leadership, an ethical system derived largely from the Calvinism[1] of his Scottish background, were spread through the lectures *On Heroes and Hero Worship,* the semi-historical theorizing in *Past and Present,* and elsewhere. His impressive style and confident (though often inconsistent) opinions strongly stimulated many younger writers. In philosophy he attacked the rationalism and empiricism of a scientific and industrial epoch and pioneered for the German "idealism" of [Immanuel] Kant and [Georg Wilhelm Friedrich] Hegel, with its emphasis on the human mind and spirit as the creating and controlling force in our existence.

The school of thought which Carlyle opposed had been set up in England by Jeremy Bentham and James Mill, and was led by the latter's son, John Stuart Mill, whose *Logic* was a landmark of 1843. Its influence reached into practically every branch of thinking. In political theory it was known as "Utilitarianism," based on the concept that the advisability of any procedure should be determined by the general welfare ("the greatest happiness of the greatest number") rather than by abstract principles. This doctrine obviously carried implications of grave significance to the whole realm of ethics.

---

1. the religious doctrines of John Calvin, emphasizing the omnipotence of God and the salvation of the elect by God's grace alone

In philosophy, the equivalent system was "Positivism," which insisted that the only acceptable material for consideration is provided by experience, without regard to metaphysical theories and deductive reasoning. Religion fell under this ban, and accordingly most of the utilitarians and positivists were "free-thinkers," though few of them took the outright stand of skepticism or atheism. About 1870 Thomas Henry Huxley proposed the word *agnostic* to describe their point of view, indicating that they regarded the immaterial concepts of the existence of God and the immortality of the human soul as being beyond any possible power of proof, either negative or affirmative. . . .

PHILOSOPHY MERGED WITH THEOLOGY AND SCIENCE

Philosophical writing merged on one side into theology, on the other side into science. The writing which dealt with religion was partly concerned with the conflicting opinions within the Church of England, first brought to a focus by the *Tracts for the Times* between 1833 and 1841. A leading contributor was John Henry Newman, and he went on to a series of important and beautifully written books, especially the *Apologia Pro Vita Sua.* The other strong tendency, toward "higher criticism" and a rational interpretation of the scriptures, was also centered in a publication by a group of authors, *Essays and Reviews* (1860). The influence of Kantian philosophy was brought into the situation by a disciple of Carlyle, Frederick Denison Maurice. He, in turn, was part of the "Christian Socialist" movement which included Charles Kingsley, and it was Kingsley's onslaught upon Newman's conversion to the Roman Catholic church which evoked Newman's *Apologia.* Into this confused campaign of opposing forces Matthew Arnold stepped with his calm and apparently objective analysis of religious concepts in *Literature and Dogma* and *St. Paul and Protestantism.*

On the other side of philosophy, many of the great scientists were writing books so vivid in their material and so exciting in the novelty of their theories that they were read widely by the general public, and they strongly influenced the thinking of writers in other fields. There were also able "popularizers" who helped to arouse interest and to give the necessary elementary knowledge. . . .

Great scientists who wrote books that were works of literature as well as being scientific treatises included Sir

Charles Lyell *(Principles of Geology,* 1830–33), Charles Darwin *(The Origin of Species,* 1859, *The Descent of Man,* 1871), Alfred Russel Wallace, Thomas Henry Huxley, and John Tyndall. Later in the century, as scientific research turned from geology and zoölogy toward the study of the human being, the important figures were Sir Francis Galton, whose studies in heredity provided material for the novelists, and Sir James G. Frazer, author of a great anthropological study of primitive religion, *The Golden Bough,* a mine of strange stories and symbols for recent poets.

THE POPULARITY OF TRAVEL BOOKS

Sometimes closely connected with works on science, at other times more concerned with social conditions and international politics, were the numerous and successful books of travel. Several of the great scientists thus gave the public a glimpse into their adventures: Darwin's *Voyage of the Beagle* became a classic, and Alfred Russel Wallace wrote equally vividly in *Travels on the Amazon and Rio Negro* and *The Malay Archipelago.* The archaeologists, too, could combine scientific research with exciting experiences, as Sir Austen Henry Layard did in his books about his excavations at Nineveh.

There were areas of the world still which were new and dangerous, so that the records of the explorers had all the fascination of the unfamiliar and the thrill of peril, as well as the satisfaction of solving mysteries. Some of these explorer-authors became popular heroes, such as Sir Richard F. Burton, who wrote a breath-taking account of his visit to Mecca disguised as a Moslem pilgrim, David Livingstone, the great missionary-explorer of Central Africa, and Henry M. Stanley. Later came Charles Montagu Doughty, with his magnificently-written *Travels in Arabia Deserta.*

Just as much interest and enthusiasm, however, went into narratives of travel in near and familiar lands. In the earlier Victorian years a procession of English authors crossed the Atlantic to the United States, and usually aroused controversy on both sides of the ocean by the reports that they published. Mrs. Frances Trollope and Captain Marryat were among the first to deal with the subject; and then [Charles] Dickens, with his *American Notes,* evoked especial acrimony because of his eminence as a novelist. Dickens wrote also *Pictures from Italy.* . . .

WORKS ON ECONOMIC, POLITICAL, AND SOCIAL PHILOSOPHY

Many of the travel books imply the lively public interest in social conditions, governmental systems, and so on, which was part of the rapid growth of the "social sciences." The books on economic and political theories were important for their influence upon the writings of poets and novelists, as well as for their effect upon the thinking of the public and its translation into political action. The writers on these subjects were in their turn affected by the developments taking place in national and international affairs. Hence, some of the leading authors changed their opinions considerably with the lapse of time. . . .

John Stuart Mill, for instance, began as the spokesman for the Utilitarians, and their creed of laissez-faire capitalistic enterprise was developed in his *Principles of Political Economy* (1848). His wider sympathies, however, began to show in his essay *On Liberty*, ten years later, and his *Representative Government*, and eventually his views were not far from Socialism. . . .

Mill's thinking was closer to the actual political trends of England and the United States for the past century, but his chilly reasoning had less appeal to readers than Carlyle's eloquent denunciations and exhortations. When Carlyle began to express his ideas of social philosophy he produced such an odd mixture of discussion and fiction in *Sartor Resartus*—a kind of novel without a plot—that publishers scorned the book. As his style became more and more eccentric the public gradually learned to like it, even though he irritated most people by his contemptuous attitude toward all their shibboleths.[2] In *Past and Present* he idealized the handicrafts and the paternalism of the middle ages in contrast with the greed and mass-production of the competitive system. *Latter-day Pamphlets* showed the full extent of his reactionary ferocity; and later *Shooting Niagara—and After* was his attack upon the Reform Bill of 1867. He condemned Mill's economics as "the dismal science" because it implied that human beings were helpless slaves of economic forces.

THE WORKS OF JOHN RUSKIN AND MATTHEW ARNOLD

The leading convert to Carlyle's beliefs was John Ruskin. Beginning as a rich business man's son and a scholarly critic

2. favorite causes and ideas

of art, Ruskin seemed anything but a person to become concerned over social controversies. While writing his books on art history, *The Seven Lamps of Architecture* and *Stones of Venice*, he gradually developed his theory that great art can be produced only in conditions of freedom and self-respect. The drab life of the industrial cities and the ugly products of the factory convinced him that his own era lacked these conditions. His other important book on art, *Modern Painters*, brought him into touch with the Pre-Raphaelite movement[3] and strengthened his love for the middle ages. When these views brought him into the camp of Carlyle he began to write on economic subjects.

Ruskin's literary style had been much admired for its careful and elaborate constructions and for its passages of richly poetic description. When he undertook to expound economics he schooled himself in a clear and simple manner of expression which proved effective for its purpose. *Unto This Last* and *Munera Pulveris* aroused such opposition when they appeared as serials in magazines that the editors discontinued them. In these books, *The Two Paths, Fors Clavigera,* and others, Ruskin revealed his movement toward a definitely socialistic creed. His analysis of social problems was often mingled with rather naïve ethical moralizing, but to his own time he was eminently successful in awakening social concern among an influential and idealistic class of readers. . . .

It is a paradoxical fact that the violent and sometimes incoherent ideas of Carlyle, springing from his intuitive hatred of industrial capitalism, when harnessed to a more analytical study of economic problems by Ruskin, and tried out in practice by [William] Morris, helped to father the English Fabian Socialist group, which allied itself with the Labor movement to become a political party, and in 1946 took over the actual remodeling of the English way of life.

Standing apart from these angry theorists, but just as deeply concerned over the materialism and the uncouthness of the time, was Matthew Arnold. With his lucid prose and restrained irony he tried to bring some reason and perspective to bear on the disputes. Just as he wrote his literary essays in the hope of making English readers aware of the currents of

3. painters and writers who advanced the style and spirit of Italian painting before Raphael; that is, to infuse art with moral qualities through a study of nature and the depiction of uplifting subjects

world literature, and wrote *Literature and Dogma* to propose a moderate form of religious faith which might survive in a scientific era because it dispensed with miracles and biblical infallibility, so in *Culture and Anarchy* he recommended the virtues of "sweetness and light" to replace the heat and confusion that swirled about him. As often happens to conciliators, he annoyed most of the factions; but his gift of phrase-making contributed to the language several permanent epithets, such as "Philistine"[4] and "Hellenism."[5] The later years of the century produced no writer on social, political, or economic theory of stature to rival those already mentioned. . . .

HISTORICAL WRITINGS

Alongside of the other social sciences, history was prominent in Victorian literature. The most admired historian in the earlier half of the era was Thomas Babington Macaulay, who set a fashion for a picturesque narrative style, full of vivid details, modeled upon the techniques of the historical novel. His series of "Essays" in the *Edinburgh Review,* though ostensibly book reviews, were actually short historical studies, and his practice in them led to his large work, *The History of England,* which occupied the last fifteen years of his life. Its five large volumes covered only the years 1680 to 1700. Its sound construction, careful detail, and easy but dignified style made it immensely popular. Almost alone among the leading authors he represented the prevailing political and social tone of the age—the complacent approval of material progress and the optimistic liberalism of the Whig party. Accordingly his writing was free from the agonized protests and from the groping but sometimes profound search for meaning which marked his contemporaries. He wrote efficiently about the surface of events, and he suited the temper of his readers so well that his anti-Tory interpretation of English history prevailed almost unchallenged in England and the United States for generations.

In the same years as Macaulay, Carlyle was also devoting himself principally to history. He carried even further the use of fictional methods to heighten the vividness and dramatic intensity of his narrative, giving the reader a sense of immediate observation of the scenes depicted. [American

4. a smug, ignorant, especially middle-class person who is regarded as being indifferent or antagonistic to artistic and cultural values   5. the civilization and culture of ancient Greece

writer Ralph Waldo] Emerson termed the effect "stereoscopic." Carlyle's theory of "the hero" made him assert that "the history of what man has accomplished in this world is at bottom the History of the Great Men who have worked here." His first historical masterpiece, *The French Revolution*, was a joint biography of a group of leaders. His later and even more gigantic works, on [English military, political, and religious leader Oliver] Cromwell and Frederick the Great [king of Prussia 1740–1786], were only slightly less picturesque because the subject-matter was not so violent. Carlyle based his histories on such full research that neither his eccentricities of style nor his prejudiced opinions could seriously affect their essential value. The more academic historians wrote thorough and readable books, though none rivaled the artistic skill of Macaulay and Carlyle. . . .

A DEARTH OF BIOGRAPHY AND AUTOBIOGRAPHY

In spite of Carlyle's enthusiasm for biography, this branch of historical writing did not flourish among the Victorians. Countless large volumes of "Life and Letters" were published, but these were of the "official testimonial" type, usually written by amateurs or literary hacks. . . .

The "short biography" was not clearly recognized during the Victorian period as a distinct literary form; but circumstances produced some examples of it. Macaulay's essays often assumed this form, and it was used in Carlyle's *Heroes* lectures and in [William Makepeace] Thackeray's two lecture series, *The English Humorists* and *The Four Georges*. Later in the century many historians and critics wrote articles of this type for the magazines and collected them into volumes, such as Leslie Stephen's *Studies of a Biographer* and Walter Bagehot's *Biographical Studies*.

Autobiography was not conspicuous in the Victorian age. Though almost all the writers expressed their personal ideas and often revealed their characters while doing so, they seldom chose their own lives as the ostensible subject. Newman's *Apologia* is a conspicuous exception; but it too was intended to be a vehicle for controversy, and did not undertake a balanced account of the author's whole career. Probably the best autobiography, strangely enough, was that of the reticent John Stuart Mill. Ruskin covered the first half of his own life rather unevenly in *Praeterita;* and Carlyle's *Reminiscences*, published after his death, were also incomplete. . . .

No Victorian Personal Essays

Perhaps the same reasons which caused the dearth of good autobiography were also responsible for the almost total absence of a more distinctly literary *genre*, the personal essay. During the Romantic generation this had been the outstanding type of prose; and the continued expansion of the magazines gave wide opportunity for the publication of such essays in the Victorian age. Two forces, however, militated against it. One was the intellectual seriousness of the time; most of the writers mentioned in this section were so deeply concerned with argument and demonstration that the informal essay would have seemed to them to be trivial and pointless. The other foe of the essay was the novel. Some of Dickens's *Sketches by Boz* were in the tradition of [Charles] Lamb and [William] Hazlitt, but he soon discovered that in fiction he could make more profitable use of his material. Thackeray was by nature cut out to be an essayist. His *Paris Sketch Book, Book of Snobs,* and many other writings during the first ten years of his career were of this type; and after making his fortune with novels he returned happily to essay-writing in *The Roundabout Papers,* which are the best Victorian example of the true informal essay. The only other mid-Victorian who could achieve quite the subtle blend of humor, pathos, sympathy, and irony was Thackeray's Scottish friend, Dr. John Brown, author of *Horae Subsecivae* and *Rab and His Friends.*

In the last quarter of the century the traditional informal essay was brought back to prominence by another Scotsman, Robert Louis Stevenson, who had enough leisure to be thoughtful without wishing to be instructive; and from that time onward the essay flourished. A special category, the "nature essay," was best represented by Richard Jefferies. Oscar Wilde, in *Intentions,* wrote witty, paradoxical essays; Andrew Lang wrote urbane ones; Alice Meynell wrote fastidious ones. Most of the late-Victorian essayists, however, were dealing chiefly with literary topics.

CHAPTER 3

The Poets

Victorian Poetry Reflects the Intellectual Uncertainty of the Age

Kristian Smidt

Kristian Smidt argues that Victorian poets—especially Alfred Tennyson, Robert Browning, and Matthew Arnold—were deprived of the philosophical certainty that characterized the poetry of the Romantic age. The Victorian world was constantly in flux; challenges provided by science to the traditional truths of religion left Victorian poets without a consistent worldview. Poets such as Tennyson and Browning wrote about the unsettling nature of change, but, as Smidt concludes, their poetry lacked a prophetic quality and their message became tedious. Kristian Smidt taught English literature at the University of Oslo. He is the author of *Books and Men: A Short History of English and American Literature* and *Poetry and Belief in the Work of T.S. Eliot*.

There was probably just as much philosophy and metaphysics in the English poetry of the seventeenth and eighteenth centuries as in that of the nineteenth. But the thinking of the Victorian poets was different in kind from that of their predecessors, barring perhaps the Romanticists. When [John] Milton set out to 'justify the ways of God to men', the assumption was that he actually possessed sufficient knowledge to do so. And [Alexander] Pope in the eighteenth century echoed Milton's assurance as well as his words in wishing to 'vindicate the ways of God to Man'. The Victorian poets made no such claims, or if they did it was in a totally different spirit. Theirs not to expound and teach but to question why and how and what.

Characteristically the poetry of the Victorian period deals with a search or quest—for knowledge or for something sym-

Excerpted from Kristian Smidt, "The Intellectual Quest of Victorian Poets," *English Studies*, April 1959. Copyright © Swets & Zeitlinger Publishers. Reprinted with permission.

bolising knowledge and certainty. The ubiquity of the theme could be proved by examples from a great variety of works and writers. Tennyson's Ulysses is the representative figure,

> yearning in desire
> To follow knowledge like a sinking star
> Beyond the utmost bound of human thought.

Or another of Tennyson's figures, Sir Galahad, riding on and on in search of the Holy Grail. There is Browning's Paracelsus, seeking

> to comprehend the works of God
> And God himself, and all God's intercourse
> With the human mind; . . .

There is Matthew Arnold, recognising

> an unspeakable desire
> After the knowledge of our buried life,
> A thirst to spend our fire and restless force
> In tracking out our true, original course;
> A longing to inquire
> Into the mystery of this heart that beats
> So wild, so deep in us, to know
> Whence our thoughts come and where they go.
>
> ('The Buried Life.')

WRITERS CHOOSE POETRY FOR THEIR SEARCH

. . . Why, one may ask, having such problems to grapple with, did not these poets speculate in discursive prose and in philosophical language rather than in the surely recalcitrant medium of verse? Why did they not turn philosophers and do the thing systematically?

Only one answer is possible. They were dedicated men. They had a prophetic mission. . . .

[Romantic poet Percy Bysshe] Shelley, it will be remembered, concluded his *Defence of Poetry* by hymning the mystic powers of the poet:

> It is impossible to read the compositions of the most celebrated writers of the present day without being startled with the electric life which burns within their words. They measure the circumference and sound the depths of human nature with a comprehensive and all-penetrating spirit, and they are themselves perhaps the most sincerely astonished at its manifestations; for it is less their spirit than the spirit of the age. Poets are the hierophants[1] of an unapprehended inspiration; the mirrors of the gigantic shadows which futurity casts

1. interpreters of sacred mysteries

upon the present; the words which express what they understand not; the trumpets which sing to battle, and feel not what they inspire; the influence which is moved not, but moves. Poets are the unacknowledged legislators of the world.

Anyone taking such views seriously and feeling that he had the gift of poetic inspiration must inevitably come to rely on poetry, including his own, to express true insight and understanding even if his thought was ordinarily bewildered. Shelley's *Defence* was not published till 1840, but his ideas were well known and there can be no doubt that the Victorian poets consciously accepted the prophet's mantle which he laid on their shoulders. They still felt that the poets were the philosophical leaders of mankind and its intellectual pioneers: '. . . but now / I shall be priest and prophet as of old', says the speaker of [Robert Browning's] 'Pauline'. The philosophers proper might work out elaborate systems and publish them in learned volumes, but only the poets could bring out the central significance of their ideas and relate them to the times, turning them into beliefs and ideals for men of the nineteenth century and for their children.

But the Victorians inherited the enthusiasm of the romantic revolt without the possibility of repeating the grandiose negations and prophetic assertions of such as Shelley. For the intellectual climate was now more argumentative. It was no use now producing 'words which express what they understand not'—when they did the words were in danger of expressing nothing at all, as Browning was to discover. Thoughts in this new age of science had to be precise and understandable, not 'trumpets which sing to battle and feel not what they inspire'. It was all very well for Shelley to speak of 'electric life', but now 'electric light' was on its way. The impact of the French Revolution, which had been felt so blissfully by the romantics, had died down, and instead there was the continuing but far more prosaic impulse of the Industrial Revolution. Jeremy Bentham's utilitarian pamphlets had succeeded [William] Godwin's imaginative *Political Justice*. Poetic intuition was fighting against heavy odds.

POETS STRUGGLE WITH NEW CHALLENGES FROM SCIENCE

The Victorian age was one of those which met a challenge to accepted beliefs only comparable to the intellectual upheaval which occurred in the late Renaissance. . . . Charles Darwin's challenge coincided with the direct challenge to religious beliefs represented by the Higher Criticism.[2] In all fields at the same time science and scientific philosophy were clamorous for attention. Thus the first popular exposé of evolutionary theory, Robert Chambers's *Vestiges of the Natural History of Creation*, as well as George Eliot's translation of [German critic David Friedrich] Strauss's rationalistic *Leben Jesu* and John Stuart Mill's positivistic *System of Logic* were all of them published in the eighteen-forties.

Belief in anything intangible and undemonstrable was made increasingly difficult, it was felt, by the advance of science. Fact was taking the place of faith. Even dreams were made impossible by the encroachment of fact, as Tennyson had complained as early as 1829, when he wrote his Cambridge prize poem 'Timbuctoo'. He first sees Timbuctoo in a Utopian dream as a city of mysterious loveliness. But then reality takes hold of his spirit and Discovery reveals the city for what it is:

> Black specks amid a waste of dreary sand,
> Low-built, mud-wall'd, Barbarian settlements,
> How chang'd from this fair City!

... It is sometimes said that the death of Tennyson's friend Arthur Hallam, in 1833, was the event which mainly plunged the young poet into the metaphysical despair which is recorded in 'In Memoriam'. But his struggles had begun several years before Hallam died and were struggles of doctrinal faith against the onslaught of sceptical rationalism. Hallam's death naturally intensified the conflict and added great emotional force to it, but was hardly the cause. Nor was it responsible for its fundamentally intellectual character, which is also displayed in 'The Two Voices', the poetic dialogue written just after the bereavement.

A similar struggle of the old-world faith to survive may be found in Browning. Though his childhood beliefs proved more resilient than Tennyson's, he felt throughout his life the restless 'craving after knowledge' of his speaker in 'Pauline'.

No one, however, felt the conflict more agonisingly than Matthew Arnold, grown up under the influence of his remarkable father, Thomas Arnold of Rugby,[3] whom he admired but could not follow. Thomas Arnold was a liberal Broad-Church man, but he knew his own mind in matters of

---

2. historical and interpretive criticism of the Bible which treated the Old Testament not as divinely inspired books but as a kind of Hebrew library of human documents
3. Thomas Arnold was headmaster of the highly respected Rugby School.

belief and he was a stickler for discipline. Matthew, growing up somewhat later than Tennyson and Browning, neither knew his own mind nor had any relish for authority. His intellectual plight is poignantly expressed in 'Stanzas from the Grande Chartreuse', where, thinking of his lost faith, he speaks of himself as

> Wandering between two worlds, one dead,
> The other powerless to be born,
> With nowhere yet to rest my head,

So the poets were left with the intellectual task, much more exacting perhaps than any that Shelley tackled, of writing poetry while trying to piece together a belief and a world view that should take adequate account of the assertions of scientists and positivists.[4] They could no longer liberate their minds in revolutionary ardour, but were pressed to argue their beliefs and disbeliefs. There was a desperate need for certainty, to reconcile faith and knowledge in a higher enlightenment.

POETS RESPOND TO EVOLUTION

In particular, the poets could not remain indifferent to the theories of Evolution, and their various responses to these theories form one of the most interesting chapters of the intellectual and literary history of the age. . . . There are many indications in Tennyson's later poetry, however, that when he came to know Darwin's theory of natural selection with its emphasis on blind chance in the struggle for survival he lost much of his zest for Evolution. And as time went on he felt more and more acutely how slow and haphazard a process it was bound to be. There was a new crisis of faith. . . .

The development from optimism to anxiety or even fear in relation to evolutionary ideas certainly seems an important strand in Tennyson's poetic woof.

If we turn to Browning, we shall find that he never accepted the idea that biological evolution would go on and on. The bodies of men and animals, he thought, had reached complete development with the appearance of man:

> And man appears at last. So far the seal
> Is put on life; one stage of being complete,
>
> ('Paracelsus.')

4. any of several viewpoints that stress attention to actual practice over consideration of what is abstract and ideal

It only remains for man, and man alone, to continue developing his spiritual nature:

> the body sprang
> At once to the height, and stayed, but the soul,—no!
> ('A Death in the Desert.')

. . . Browning characteristically sees the world as a place of trial and preparation. And after 'Paracelsus' he quite consistently saw the Creator as transcendent, not immanent: 'Externe / Not inmost, is the Cause, fool!' ('Francis Furini'). He even tried to assure himself that the questing intellect ought not to venture too far:

> where and when and how?
> Leave that to the First Cause! Enough that now,
> Here where I stand, this moment's me and mine,
> Shows me what is, permits me to divine
> What shall be.

Although these are the words of the dramatic character Francis Furini, the idea which they express can be found in numerous places in Browning's poetry.

There is little change in the larger philosophical implications of that poetry after 'Paracelsus'. In important respects it is determinedly and even refreshingly counter-evolutionary. This may seem surprising considering the age and Browning's usual optimism. But the only really surprising aspect of his philosophy as well as the only notable development of his thought, it seems to me, is in the idea which he gradually came to entertain of a continued spiritual and moral evolution in the hereafter. His Rabbi Ben Ezra enjoys a period of rest and understanding in old age before death sends him to a new sphere of evolutionary struggle:

> And I shall thereupon
> Take rest, ere I be gone
> Once more on my adventure brave and new:
> Fearless and unperplexed
> When I wage battle next,
> What weapons to select, what armour to indue.

This is indeed a rather startling picture of heaven, but it shows that Browning in at least one respect—that of spiritual growth—was more evolutionary than any other poet. . . .

THE THEMES OF CHANGE AND DOUBT WEAR THIN

Even if the poets came to believe in some form of evolution, however, they had hardly solved their philosophical problems. For a belief in change and growth alone can hardly be a final philosophical standpoint. . . .

Perhaps if the Victorians had been more clear-sighted, or if they had been more fortunate in their intellectual environment and stimuli, they might have found an answer to satisfy both philosophy and poetry. Some exciting new time concept might have worked the miracle—such as the idea that time, instead of flowing on and on with its burden of change and development without any apparent goal was only a dimension of our habitual experience and might itself be contained within a larger dimension which was timeless. [Thomas] Carlyle had some such intuition in *Sartor Resartus* and wrote poetically enough about it:

> Pierce through the Time-element, glance into the Eternal. Believe what thou findest written in the sanctuaries of Man's Soul, even as all Thinkers, in all ages, have devoutly read it there: that Time and Space are not God, but creations of God; that with God as it is a universal HERE, so is it an everlasting NOW.

An ancient idea, of course, as Carlyle himself points out, and one which, in its general mystical form, was quite familiar to the Victorians. . . .

It was a pity that the prophets were not better served by their inspiration. But perhaps they never really had sufficient faith in their oracular poetic medium, in the ability of poetry to turn their benighted thoughts into supernatural clarity. Arnold the critic might declare that 'More and more mankind will discover that we have to turn to poetry to interpret life for us, to console us, to sustain us.' To Arnold writing in prose, poetry was 'an ever surer and surer stay'. But what of Arnold the poet? And what of Tennyson and Browning?

Both Tennyson and Browning, especially the latter, somewhat distrusted poetry and the romantic-intellectual conception of poetry, never being entirely convinced of its adequacy to deal with the most important problems of life. . . .

Naturally Browning recognised the value of poetry and art, witness all the artists of various kinds included in his portrait gallery. [Italian painter] Fra Lippo Lippi is an eloquent defender of the high function of art:

> we're made so that we love
> First when we see them painted, things we have passed
> Perhaps a hundred times nor cared to see;
> And so they are better, painted—better to us.
> Which is the same thing. Art was given for that;

God uses us to help each other so,
Lending our minds out.

But nevertheless, Browning always sees life as superior to poetry. He quotes himself in 'Development' as habitually saying that 'No dream's worth waking'. Poetry, he admits in 'The Last Ride Together', is 'something, nay 'tis much'—'but then', he goes on to ask the poet,

Have you yourself what's best for men?
Are you—poor, sick, old ere your time—
Nearer one whit your own sublime
Than we who never have turned a rhyme?
Sing, riding's a joy! For me, I ride.

. . . So, of the two great prophets of Victorian poetry, one, Tennyson, doubted his message, and the other, Browning, had doubts of his medium. And they went on doubting too long. The Victorian age itself was too long. Once its initial challenge had been caught up, it settled down to a long process of uneasy adaptation, which lasted through the 1860's and 70's and 80's and 90's without any new intellectual upheavals of the first order to goad or stimulate the poets into rising on stepping-stones of their dead selves to higher things.

Great poets should die young if they cannot renew themselves or be renewed. But Tennyson and Browning both lived on into a ripe old age and certainly survived their own best efforts. Critics are right in detecting a certain hollowness at least in their later poetry. Not the poets' affirmations and beliefs were hollow, however,—it was their doubts which had become mechanical gestures and for that reason perhaps insincere. Poetry let them down if they had ever believed with Shelley that it would do their thinking and prophesying for them. They spoke their doubts into its oracular orifice and it was still their doubts that came out, though sometimes in beautiful clouds of aromatic smoke, at the public end. But one cannot just go on doubting and remain a poet. And so the great age ended, not with a bang and not quite with a whimper, but with something indeterminately in between.

Having recognised this hollow sound towards the end of the period, we must still insist on the basic sincerity of the Victorian giants of poetry. They genuinely wrestled with intellectual problems and turned their struggles into art. They wrote verse because they were poets. Even Arnold was too much of a poet not to throw his speculations into verse. But they did not just happen to be poets *and* intellectual seekers, or poets who had lost their intellectual bearings. Poetry offered itself to them as a natural vehicle of thought because their intellectual dilemma was also an *emotional* one. I do not now mean emotional in the sense that the death of friends, or other events that touched them closely caused metaphysical distress. I mean that beliefs and ideas themselves necessarily have an emotional aspect. The attachment to an idea, like the attachment to a person, is itself an emotion, which will be coloured by the kind of idea to which one is attached and which will sometimes be passionate. Further, it is emotionally reassuring simply to be able to believe in certain things at all; and the loss of once comforting beliefs may be very hard to endure. As Harold says in Tennyson's 'Promise of May':

> Sometimes I wonder
> When man has surely learnt at last that all
> His old-world faith, the blossom of his youth,
> Has faded, falling fruitless—whether then
> All of us, all at once, may not be seized
> With some fierce passion, not so much for Death
> As against Life!

The poets, then, were concerned not only with speculating upon what they could or could not believe in, but with expressing, as [poet and critic] T.S. Eliot would say, how it felt to be uncertain. The feeling of intellectual vacillation, as a matter of fact, is one that poetry can probably express far better than prose because it can present two alternative points of view as simultaneously attractive to the same mind.

Victorian Poets Were Devalued

Walter E. Houghton and G. Robert Stange

Walter E. Houghton and G. Robert Stange describe the confusion surrounding Victorian poets as they tried to identify their role and function. According to the authors, the reading public and the utilitarian reformers placed little value on poetry, an attitude which left poets isolated from the public and from each other. In their alienation they were torn between devotion to their individual expression and to their public duty and were confused by an audience that ignored them on one hand and on the other demanded that they be prophets and guides. Both authors taught English: Walter E. Houghton at Wellesley College in Massachusetts and G. Robert Stange at the University of Minnesota. Houghton is coeditor of a two-volume anthology entitled *British Literature*. Stange is the author of *Poetry of Coleridge* and *Matthew Arnold: The Poet as Humanist* and editor of *The Cambridge Editions of Tennyson and Browning*.

To discuss the general characteristics of any age of English poetry is to deal with the whole of an intricate organism. Every generalization will lead us to what we conveniently call "background"—to social changes, intellectual movements, and the sociology of literature. Any general description will be dangerous unless it is tested against the experience of the literature itself, and unless it is understood that it can do no more than help to focus certain lines and tendencies, certain clusters of qualities, or at best to provoke a fresh reading and an original response.

In the case of Victorian poetry a synthetic view may seem more than usually absurd. Multiplicity and extreme variety

Excerpted from Walter E. Houghton and G. Robert Stange, *Victorian Poetry and Poetics* (Boston: Houghton Mifflin, 1959). Copyright ©1959 by Walter E. Houghton and G. Robert Stange.

of style and belief are the principal characteristics of the period. There are so many different attitudes toward diction, subject matter, imagery, and tone that a reader despairs of finding any common features. Yet this heterogeneity is in itself a characteristic, and if one contrasts the significant poetry written between 1830 and 1900 with the poetry which preceded and followed it, certain distinctive traits are thrown into perspective.

THE POSITION AND FUNCTION OF THE POET WAS IN DOUBT

Any consideration of Victorian poetry must begin with the question of the position and function of the poet, since the effect of this question on the character of literature assumed a peculiar importance in that age. At first sight, a Victorian poet would seem to have enjoyed unique advantages, for widening public education and the extension of political and social power to the middle classes provided him with a larger potential audience than any writer had yet had. In the years after 1830, critics, journalists, and ordinary citizens bestowed on the poet the role of prophet, and paid excessive tribute to his power for social good. Yet these seeming advantages were the contributing factors to the profound uncertainty as to the poetic function which perplexed the work of every great Victorian. The problem of communication, the split between the poet and his audience, the alienation of the poet—all these literary diseases of our own time were first suffered by the Victorian writers.

In the earlier eighteenth century the merits of a particular poet might be disputed, but the function of poetry did not require definition. The great ages of Greek and Roman literature provided a standard against which both poet and reader were willing to match the writings of their own time. The poet's audience was limited and, in terms of essential beliefs and values, reassuringly homogeneous. [Alexander] Pope might rail against false taste, the supremacy of dunces, the iniquity of the times, but it is obvious that the expectations of his audience harmonized with his interests and capacities. Poet and reader belonged to an undivided realm of the "literate" and "well-bred"; the social and moral value of the poet's function and—most significant in the light of later events—the validity of imaginative language were not seriously questioned.

By the 1830's, when [Alfred] Tennyson emerged as a significant figure, this cultural stability no longer existed. In the early years of the nineteenth century, before any of the Victorian poets had begun their careers, critics were predicting a dark and brief future for poetry. In 1818 the great Romantic critic, William Hazlitt, observed that "the progress of knowledge and refinement has a tendency to clip the wings of poetry. The province of the imagination is principally visionary. . . . Hence the history of religious and poetical enthusiasm is much the same, and both have received a sensible shock from the progress of experimental philosophy." This notion that poetry would wither away as the natural sciences developed was more fully expressed in young [Thomas Babington] Macaulay's famous essay on [John] Milton (1825). Macaulay . . . considered that "as civilization advances, poetry almost necessarily declines." The visionary and particularizing faculties of poetic language seemed to him to be inconsistent with the generalizing and theoretical language of a scientific age; the men of his century would, he said, make progressively "better theories and worse poems."

Such positivistic views are still with us. We need not be concerned either to defend or attack them; it is sufficient to note their influence. Macaulay was one of the most cultivated men of his age, yet he expressed no particular regret at this predicted disappearance of poetic speech—of what had been for centuries regarded as the noblest language of man. If the learned and humane Macaulay could coolly herald the disappearance of poetry, the partially educated were likely to be completely unconcerned. A large segment of the new, wide audience was chiefly engaged in gaining control of material forces, and judged the value of both literature and speculative activity by their possible application to productive use. For the most part, it must be said, the incompatibility of the languages of poetry and of science was affirmed, not by genuine scientists, but by writers who had only a vague knowledge of scientific procedures. However, so great a biologist as Charles Darwin observed late in life that his researches had effected in him a loss of the "higher aesthetic tastes," and that he was dead to the pleasures of art. Indeed, the feeling he described seems to have been widespread among the intelligentsia. At the time that Tennyson first appeared in print, a critic writing in the most influential literary journal of the period said, "It now requires a very high and lofty spirit to command attention to poetry. . . . There is in the world just as much poetic power and poetic capacity as ever, but poetry is not talked about. . . . People nowadays do not see the *use* of poetry, and there is a general opinion got abroad, that nothing is valuable that is not useful."[1]

THE EFFECTS OF UTILITARIAN VALUES

It was not only the growth of the natural sciences that had the effect of perplexing received opinions as to the value of poetry and the poet's function. The most significant tendencies of the time in political and economic life, philosophy, and religion also led either to a minimization of or an outright hostility to poetry. The new reading public created by the spread of social advantages disconcerted the poets by displaying untraditional—and unpredictable—attitudes and responses. The industrial system created, among other things, the type of the tired businessman, unashamedly unwilling to give time to the vaporings of poetry, impatient with endeavors that did not contribute to material advance. Utilitarian philosophy tended either to ignore poetry altogether or to deplore it as a species of fiction that impeded rational perception. The strict Evangelicals[2] considered secular literature a snare of the senses tempting man away from the rigorous path of duty and righteousness.

All the literature of the early Victorian period is informed by a peculiar distress. Whatever their beliefs, serious writers shared a conviction that new modes of thought and behavior called all in doubt. A close friend of Tennyson's, Richard Trench, expressed a view that may well have been Tennyson's own: "When, except in our time," he asked, "did men seek to build up their poetry on their own individual experiences instead of some objective foundations common to all men?" He defined a condition that produced poetry full of aberrance and uncertainty; there is no common level to Victorian poetry, no ceiling of taste and judgment that might restrain excess. Certainly before the nineteenth century there were no poets of a stature comparable to Tennyson's or Browning's whose poetry touched such extremes of goodness and badness. And yet—the qualification must be immediately made—unevenness and the tendency to go off on

1. based on Jeremy Bentham's philosophy called Utilitarianism   2. a religious sect that had broken away from the traditional Church of England

various lines make for great strengths as well as weaknesses in the poetry of the period.

The multiplicity of Tennyson's work may be the result of his conscious effort to define a poetic role for himself, his sometimes anxious attempt to bring his talent into harmony with what he conceived to be the main currents of his age. In the course of his search he tried many different types of poetry, and handled at one time or another every conceivable kind of subject. Browning tried in a calculated way to find a literary manner and a means of publication by which he could reach his unknown audience—with so little success that midway in his career he protested the public indifference to his work and spoke darkly of giving up poetry altogether. Matthew Arnold, tired perhaps by the difficulties of creation in what he called a "deeply *unpoetical*" age, turned after a short career in verse to literary and social criticism. All the evidence supports the generalization of the distinguished scientist, Sir Oliver Lodge; looking back on the Victorian age, he concluded:

> Poets generally must have felt it as a terrible time. What refuge existed for a poet save to isolate himself from the turmoil, shut himself into his cabin, and think of other times and other surroundings, away from the uproar and the gale?

POETS FELT ISOLATED

The intense preoccupation of the major Victorian poets with the problem of isolation is, then, a natural result of the insecurity of their cultural status. Situations of betrayal, alienation, separation from life and love, appear in Tennyson's poetry early and late. Browning, all through his career, recurred to the cases of the artist who cannot convey his vision to a scornful citizenry, or of the lovers who, in the nature of things, cannot achieve more than superficial communication. Arnold provided many variations of his great plaint which begins:

> Yes! in the sea of life enisled
> With echoing straits between us thrown,
> Dotting the shoreless watery wild,
> We mortal millions live *alone*.

It is, of course, a note of eternal sadness that Tennyson's Mariana or Tiresias, Browning's Paracelsus, or the lover of "Two in the Campagna," and Arnold's grave young poet are meant to sound. Gerard Manley Hopkins' sonnet, "To seem

the stranger lies my lot," treats several kinds of estrangement, but significant among them is the loneliness of the
poet who has no sympathetic readers. The condition represented in these poems is not merely the state of the artist in
the age of Victoria, but the solitude in which all men everywhere live and die. Nevertheless, in no other body of poetry
has the theme of alienation assumed such prominence, and
at no other time have literary themes so closely reflected the
distresses of poetic life.

In truth, these writers were isolated—not only from the
dominant practical movements of their age, but from each
other. There is a remarkable lack of cohesion among the poets of this period. In the age of Pope, and later, in the age of
[Samuel] Johnson, writers tended to form self-sustaining
groups. The French contemporaries of the Victorians were
very conscious of belonging to a literary school from which
they could derive aid and criticism. But with the exception of
the Pre-Raphaelite Brotherhood, there was no "school," no
well-defined movement in poetry, to which a Victorian
writer could attach himself. There were in the century a
number of effective groups and impressive movements: in
addition to the Evangelicals and the Utilitarians, there were
the Oxford Movement,[3] and in politics the Anti-Corn Law
League[4] and the Young England group;[5] but it is a comment
on the condition of letters to observe that none of these had
an influential bearing on poetry. The great poets themselves
were dispersed. Tennyson and Browning were on good
terms socially, but there is no evidence that they ever had
anything important to say to each other about the practice of
their art. Arnold took a dim view of the work of Tennyson
and Browning, and apparently found the poetry of [Alger-
non] Swinburne totally repugnant. Gerard Hopkins did not
find among his poet friends a reader who understood what
he was doing.

To these atomized conditions of literary life may be due
much of the variety, the independence, the vigorous experi-
mentalism of Victorian poetry. But it is likely that the disad-
vantages of such creative conditions outweighed the advan-

3. also called Tractarianism; a Church-of-England movement formed to counteract a
perceived threat from Catholic emancipation and secular interference   4. The Corn
Laws restricted the importation of grain and made prices too high for the poor. The
Anti-Corn Law League formed to expand suffrage and thus defeat the Corn Laws.
5. a group of Tories led by Benjamin Disraeli to insure that the nobility carried out its
social responsibilities

tages. A poet working "in silence, obscurity, and solitude" (the phrase is one Tennyson applied to himself) may lack the armor needed to meet the attack of articulate philistines.[6] Tennyson, and sometimes Browning, were capable of writing poems that now seem grossly insincere in their flattery of public preconceptions. One is tempted to think that the supporting sympathy of literary peers would have prevented or made unnecessary some of these compromises by giving the poets a firmer base from which to assert the claims of individual genius.

Another significant reflection of the status of the Victorian poet is the tension that every major poet expresses between devotion to individual sensibility and commitment to the social and moral needs of the age. Such a conflict is never resolved: Tennyson, Browning, and Arnold are always saying both yes and no to these questions, and their state of mind produced a continuing dialectic, with ever-stronger assertions of the autonomy of poetry on the one hand, and of the poet's public duty on the other. The theme—and the peculiar formulation the Victorians gave to it—has been bequeathed by them to the poets of the twentieth century, who have enthusiastically explored it.

POETS TORN BETWEEN INDIVIDUALISM AND PUBLIC DUTY

The prevailing uncertainty as to the function of poetry had a remarkable effect on subject matter. In the nineteenth century we find an entirely new preoccupation on the part of poets with the subject of poetry itself. Poets had, of course, always reflected in their poetry on the techniques and aims of their art: one need only recall [Roman poet] Horace, [French poet Nicolas] Boileau, and Pope. And the Victorians wrote enough on conventional and unconventional subjects—from love to leprosy—to qualify as practitioners in any category. But, from the early nineteenth century on, the nature, meaning, process of poetry, and the conditions of the poetic life have become a major verse theme. In more than a score of poems Tennyson considered explicitly or symbolically the nature of art and of the artist. Browning wrote an equal number of poems in which he explored more deeply and objectively the dynamics of creation and the relation of

6. smug, ignorant, especially middle-class persons who are regarded as being indifferent or antagonistic to artistic and cultural values

the artist to society. Arnold, though he contemned "the dialogue of the mind with itself," wrote many poems in which
a figure of the poet speculates on the meaning and value of
his experience and art. Reflections on poetics appear in
varying degrees in the work of less representative writers.
[Thomas] Hardy and Hopkins, for example, are only occasionally concerned with the problem, but the "Aesthetic" poets[7] at the end of the century used their poetry almost as illustrations of a theory of art, and went so far as to affirm that
the experience of art was more significant than that of life.

It is relevant to our appreciation of Victorian poetry to
suggest that its preoccupation with the meaning of art has
also been continued in the poetry of our time. Our serious
poets are elaborately conscious of their technical and spiritual problems and, like the Victorians, tend to make this interest a subject of their poetry. W.H. Auden and Wallace
Stevens are the principal names that come to mind, but
every eminent poet of [the twentieth] century has tended to
justify, in his verse, the significance of his art, and to create
for himself a tradition out of which he could speak with confidence and fullness. Public hostility—or better say, indifference—to poetry is even more widespread today than it was
in the time of Tennyson, and the moderns seem to differ
from their Victorian forebears only in no longer trying to
bridge the gap which separates them from the public. At the
moment, a little past mid-century, there is a tendency for serious poetry to re-approach the common language, but for
more than half the twentieth century the conditions in
which the poet had to work have been startlingly like those
that confronted Tennyson in the 1830's.

POETS' ROLES INCONSISTENT

The final step in our definition of the status of the Victorian
poet involves an apparent inconsistency. All that has been said
about the devaluation of poets and poetry would seem to be
contradicted by the growing public emphasis on the prophetic
nature of poetry. It was a platitude of Victorian criticism that
authors were a modern priesthood whose duty was to "enlighten and encourage and purify public opinion." [Thomas]
Carlyle saluted the Man of Letters as "our most important
modern person," possessed of intuitive insight into the "True,

7. poets who rejected reform and asserted that art is for art's sake

Divine and Eternal," and therefore "the light of the world, . . . guiding it, like a sacred Pillar of Fire in its dark pilgrimage." One typical critic thought a truly great poet should be called a "Rhythmic Teacher." And a poet such as Tennyson was consulted as an oracle on matters of faith, morals, and practical politics. Too often the poets themselves accepted and promulgated this conception of their prophetic role. [William] Wordsworth and [Percy Bysshe] Shelley had called into being the Romantic Genius of the nineteenth century whose imagination was an oracular organ of truth; the doctrine was absorbed by Tennyson to such an extent that he could speak in his middle years of feeling like "a priest who can never leave the sanctuary, and whose every word must be consecrated to the service of Him who had touched his lips with the fire of heaven which was to enable him to speak in God's name to his age." Flattered by adulation (and sometimes even by commercial success—in the 1860's 65,000 copies of Tennyson's *Enoch Arden* were sold in one year) the poets were often drawn to write inflated poetry of a sort that fitted their vatic [prophetic] nature. However, even as they accepted the wreaths of laurel and roses (both literal and figurative), the greatest Victorian poets preserved a bitter distrust of their readers. Once, speaking of *In Memoriam*, Tennyson remarked that it was "the least misunderstood of all my work. I don't mean that the commentators have been more right, but that the general reading public has been less wrong than usual as to my intentions." Browning called artistry a "battle with the age / It lives in," and [George] Meredith described his audience as "the bull, the donkey and the barking cur," insisting that any poet who "follows out the vagaries of his own brain," cannot "hope for general esteem."

The promotion of poet to prophet did not involve a genuine elevation of status. Those poets who advocated a literary priesthood and were also gifted with a distinctive talent soon discovered that they had helped to build their own prisons. Bardolatry, even of the most earnest sort, limited the poet by marking out for him one particular role, a single set of values to be accepted. Though limitations of poetic autonomy have not always been harmful to the artist (have in fact sometimes stimulated a literary flowering) the Victorian paradigm of Public Poet not only deprived the artist of his independence, but denied the validity of the specifically poetic function. The tendency was to make a distinction between the "Sense of the Beautiful" and the "Sense of the Good." The prophetic poet was adjured to deny the lure of beauty and address the social and moral needs of his times. In their earnest practicality many intellectuals suppressed the ancient understanding that poetry is itself a source of value, that the ethical insights of a fine creative mind are no less profound for being embodied in the language of image rather than of sequential discourse.

Almost without exception, the most articulate supporters of the tendency to "prophetize" the poets show a notable insensitivity to the resources of poetry. In spite of his ardent praise of the Man of Letters, Carlyle, for example, was only vaguely interested in the poetry of his period, feeling that it was not the best means of achieving the work of reconstruction. Other critics, even as they praise a poet, display an exclusive interest in the edifying moral statement that can be extracted from his poem; the poetic structure they regard merely as a container for the "thought." So even though they became prophets in their own country, the fundamental insecurity of the Victorian poets was not allayed. They were like the children of rich and unloving parents, showered with gifts but essentially rejected.

Victorian Poets Accommodated Popular Taste

E.D.H. Johnson

E.D.H. Johnson argues that twentieth-century critics unfairly criticize the best Victorian writers for being too accommodating to their society's demand for reform literature. He says close analysis of their work shows that writers had a double awareness of their social function and of their own artistic integrity. In particular Johnson maintains that Alfred Tennyson, Robert Browning, and Matthew Arnold sublimated their private insights by creating their own special techniques to express them. E.D.H. Johnson has taught English at Princeton University in New Jersey. He is the editor of *The World of the Victorians: An Anthology of Prose and Poetry.*

The important writing of the Victorian period is to a large extent the product of a double awareness. This was a literature addressed with great immediacy to the needs of the age, to the particular temper of mind which had grown up within a society seeking adjustment to the conditions of modern life. And to the degree that the problems which beset the world of a century ago retain their urgency and still await solution, the ideas of the Victorian writers remain relevant and interesting to the twentieth century. Any enduring literature, however, must transcend topicality; and the critical disesteem into which so much Victorian writing has fallen may be traced to the persistent notion that the literary men of that time oversubscribed to values with which our own time is no longer in sympathy.

Excerpted from E.D.H. Johnson, *The Alien Vision of Victorian Poetry.* Copyright ©1952, renewed 1980 by Princeton University Press. Reprinted by permission of Princeton University Press.

VICTORIAN WRITERS AT ODDS WITH THEIR AGE

Yet this view ignores the fact that nearly all the eminent Victorian writers were as often as not at odds with their age, and that in their best work they habitually appealed not *to*, but *against* the prevailing mores of that age. The reader who comes to the Victorians without bias must be struck again and again by the underlying tone of unrest which pervades so much that is generally taken as typical of the period. Sooner or later he begins to wonder whether there is any such thing as a representative Victorian writer, or at any rate, whether what makes him representative is not that very quality of intransigeance as a result of which he repudiated his society and sought refuge from the spirit of the times in the better ordered realm of interior consciousness. Since, however, any tendency to exalt individual awareness at the expense of conventionally established attitudes ran counter to the concept of the role of the artist which the Victorian age tried to impose on its writers, there resulted a conflict which has been too often ignored, but which must be taken into account in reaching any satisfactory evaluation of Victorian literature. This was a conflict, demonstrable within the work of the writers themselves, between the public conscience of the man of letters who comes forward as the accredited literary spokesman of his world, and the private conscience of the artist who conceives that his highest allegiance must be to his own aesthetic sensibilities.

Most Victorian writers still thought of themselves as men of letters in the full meaning of the term. Victorian literature was predominantly a literature of ideas, and of ideas, furthermore, brought into direct relation with the daily concerns of the reading public. To a degree now inconceivable the influential literary types of the nineteenth century were expository in character—the essay, tract, and treatise. The student who wishes to understand the Victorian world begins with such works as [Thomas Carlyle's] *Past and Present*, [John Ruskin's] *The Stones of Venice*, [John Stuart Mill's] *On Liberty*, [Matthew Arnold's] *Culture and Anarchy*. The assumption that a writer's first responsibility is to get into close correspondence with his audience induced a great many of the original thinkers in the period to turn aside from their fields of special knowledge, to the end of making their theories more generally accessible. So Mill, Carlyle,

Ruskin, Arnold, [William] Morris, [Thomas] Huxley, after achieving distinction along specialized lines, gave up exclusive concentration on these in order to apply the disciplines they had mastered to subjects of the broadest human import. Or, to consider the novel, [Charles] Dickens, George Eliot, [Benjamin] Disraeli, [Charles] Kingsley, Mrs. [Elizabeth] Gaskell, and Charles Reade all quite evidently chose themes with an eye to their social significance.

SOCIETY'S DEMANDS FRUSTRATED WRITERS' ARTISTIC INTEGRITY

Yet, paradoxically, it becomes increasingly difficult to think of the great Victorians as other than solitary and unassimilated figures within their century. Deeply as they allowed themselves to be involved in the life of the times, familiarity seemed only to breed contempt. Their writings, inspired by a whole-hearted hostility to the progress of industrial culture, locate the centers of authority not in the existing social order, but within the resources of individual being. Nor was this procedure merely a reaction to the isolation which is traditionally visited on prophets without honor, although for many the years brought disillusionment and bitterness over the debacle of cherished programs of reform. The prestige of a Carlyle or Ruskin or [John Henry] Newman may almost be said to have risen in inverse proportion to the failure of their preachments. At the core of the malaise which pervades so much that is best in Victorian literature lies a sense, often inarticulate, that modern society has originated tendencies inimical to the life of the creative imagination. By mid-century the circumstances of successful literary production had begun to make demands on writers which strained to the breaking point their often very considerable capacities for compromise. Among novelists the careers of Dickens and [William Makepeace] Thackeray epitomize the all but intolerable difficulties of reconciling popular appeal with artistic integrity. A new generation, led by [Dante Gabriel] Rossetti and [Algernon] Swinburne, was to resolve the dilemma by an outspoken assertion of the artist's apartness; but for the writers who came of age in the 1830's and 1840's no such categorical disavowal of social commitment was admissible. As a result, there is recognizable in their work a kind of tension originating in the serious writer's traditional desire to communicate, but to do so without betraying the purity of

his creative motive even in the face of a public little disposed
to undergo the rigors of aesthetic experience. Even when, as
was too often the case, their love of fame overcame their
artistic restraint, traces of the initiating conflict remain
imbedded in what they wrote; and it is these constantly recurring evidences of a twofold awareness which, perhaps
more than any other trait, give its distinctive quality to the
writing of the Victorian age.

The Difficulty of Writing Midway Between the Romantics and the Pre-Raphaelites

In criticizing Victorian poetry it is necessary to keep this am-
bivalence in mind; and this is especially true for [Alfred]
Tennyson, [Robert] Browning, and Arnold, the poets who
touched their period at the greatest number of points. The
history of nineteenth-century English poetry records a gradual, but radical shift in the relationship of the artist to his
public, with the three poets just mentioned occupying a position at dead center of the forces which were in opposition.
A divorce between the artist and society first became conspicuous as an element of the Romantic movement; but even
though they had to endure abuse or neglect, the Romantics
did not in any sense think of themselves as abdicating the
poet's traditional right to speak for his age. [William] Blake,
[Samuel Taylor] Coleridge, [William] Wordsworth, [Lord]
Byron, [Percy Bysshe] Shelley, [John] Keats were all, it is
true, keenly sensitive to their generation's reluctance to pay
attention to what they were saying, but they accepted isolation as a necessary consequence of their revolutionary program. That they should confess defeat, with the alternatives
either of self-withdrawal or compromise, never seriously occurred to them. On the contrary, they declared open warfare
on the prejudices which would dispossess them and continued to assert that the poet's vision is transcendently authoritative over all other agencies of intellectual and spiritual
truth. Before the end of the century, however, the conflict
thus resolutely engaged had been lost, and the artist had
come to accept as a foregone conclusion his inefficacy as a
shaping influence on the lives of his contemporaries. In
compensation, he now espoused the aesthetic creed which
goes by the name of art for art's sake, and with [Walter] Pater and then [Oscar] Wilde as his apologists and Rossetti and
Swinburne as his models, embraced his alienation from all

but a coterie of initiates persuaded like himself to value the forms of art above its message.

Between the Romantics and the Pre-Raphaelites[1] lie Tennyson, Browning, and Arnold, leading the poetic chorus of the great Victorian noonday. And by virtue of this midway position between the two extremes represented by the schools of poetry which came before and after, their work brings into sharp focus the choice which has been forced on the modern artist. In the common view, these mid-Victorian poets, either unable or unwilling to maintain the spirit of bellicose self-sufficiency which sustained their Romantic forbears, achieved rapprochement with their audience by compromising with the middle-class morality of the time, and in so doing deliberately sacrificed artistic validity. So flagrant a betrayal of the creative impulse, the argument then continues, provoked a reaction in the following generation, whereby the pendulum swung back towards the belief that art is and must be its own justification irrespective of ulterior motive. But this version of the poetic situation in the nineteenth century gravely misrepresents the real meaning of an endeavor on which Tennyson, Browning, and Arnold were alike engaged. For each of them was ultimately seeking to define the sphere within which the modern poet may exercise his faculty, while holding in legitimate balance the rival claims of his private, aristocratic insights and of the tendencies existing in a society progressively vulgarized by the materialism of the nineteenth and twentieth centuries. Thus it came about that the double awareness, which so generally characterized the Victorian literary mind, grew almost into a perpetual state of consciousness in these poets through their efforts to work out a new aesthetic position for the artist.

TENNYSON, BROWNING, AND ARNOLD RESPOND TO DEMANDS FROM THE OUTSIDE

The literary careers of Tennyson, Browning, and Arnold present a number of striking parallels which, since their poetic endowments were so divergent, can only be explained in terms of influences impinging on them from the outside. In the early manner of each there is an introspective, even a

---

1. a group of artists and critics, Rossetti among them, who rejected the prevailing academic rules of painting; associated with the art-for-art's-sake movement

cloistral element which was later subdued in an obvious attempt to connect with contemporary currents of thought. Of the three, Tennyson succeeded most quickly in conforming to the Victorian ideal of the poet as popular bard; his reward was the laureateship as Wordsworth's successor. Browning's progress in public favor was more gradual, but the formation of the Browning Society in 1881 signalized his eventual arrival within the select company of Victorian idols of the hearth. Less versatile in poetic range, Arnold became a full-fledged man of letters and won the prestige of the Oxford Professorship of Poetry only after turning to prose; and it is perhaps worth pondering whether his inability to bring his poetry into closer accord with the demands of the age does not account for the fact that he has attracted a greater amount of serious critical attention in recent years than either Tennyson or Browning.

The Victorian writer, of course, had to acclimate himself to a reading public vastly bigger in size and more diverse and unpredictable in its literary requirements than any that had existed hitherto. There is something astonishing, even slightly appalling, in the unselective voracity with which the Victorians wolfed down [Tennyson's] *In Memoriam* and [Philip] Bailey's *Festus,* [Charles Darwin's] *The Origin of Species,* and Samuel Smiles' *Self-help,* the novels of Dickens and the tales of Harriet Martineau. The ill success of their first volumes early awakened Tennyson, Browning, and Arnold to a realization that under existing conditions originality was no passport to artistic acclaim. The critics were for the most part hostile; but it was the disapprobation of intimate friends which carried the greatest weight. For while the poets might turn a deaf ear to the voice of the age as it spoke through the weekly and monthly journals which had feebly replaced the Edinburgh and Quarterly Reviews as arbiters in literary matters, the well-intended strictures of [an Arthur] Hallam or Elizabeth Barrett or [Arthur] Clough were another matter. And friends and foes were at one in their insistence that the poets take a broader view of their responsibilities as men of letters. In general, their work drew reproof on three counts, one major and two incidental thereto. It was unduly introspective and self-obsessed, and as a result it was too often obscure in content and precious in manner. All three faults are chargeable to immaturity; but as attributed indiscriminately to Tennyson, Browning, and Arnold, they carry additional implications suggestive of the tyranny which the age was to exercise over its artists. For the invariable inference in the attacks on these poets is that their faults could easily be remedied by more attention to normal human thoughts and activities, and correspondingly by less infatuation with their own private states of being.

The experiments in the narrative and dramatic modes to which Tennyson, Browning, and Arnold turned so early in their careers were certainly undertaken out of a desire to counteract objections of this kind. Yet it is apparent from the vagaries of their critical reputations that they were never sure enough of their audience to be able to estimate its response with any degree of reliability. The appearance of [Tennyson's] *Maud* or [Browning's] *Sordello* or [Arnold's] *Empedocles on Etna*, interspersed among more admired efforts, is continuing evidence that the best will in the world could not compensate for temperamental variances with prevailing tastes which went much deeper than the authors themselves always recognized. That they should have professed impatience with the often obtuse and ill-considered estimates of their poetry is not in itself surprising; but it is to be noted that as time went on they tended increasingly to transfer this resentment to the reading public at large. In their later days Tennyson and Arnold would have agreed with Browning's statement in *Red Cotton Night-Cap Country* about "artistry being battle with the age/It lives in!" There is, of course, an element of the disingenuous in such professions of disdain for popular favor; and their assumed indifference cannot disguise the fact that all three poets were keenly sensitive to the fluctuations of their literary stock. In this respect they were no more than exhibiting an awareness natural to men of letters possessed of an inherent belief in the instrumentality of literature as a social force.

TENNYSON, BROWNING, AND ARNOLD WROTE WITH A DOUBLE AWARENESS

Yet again, the conventional explanation does not cover the facts; and we are brought back to the dichotomy which emerges from any close analysis of the relations between the artist and society in the Victorian period. The hallmark of the literary personalities of Tennyson, Browning, and Arnold alike is a certain aristocratic aloofness, a stubborn intractability which is likely to manifest itself at just those points where the contemporary social order assumed automatic conformity with its dictates. Thus, their refusal to be restricted by current suppositions is less often a subterfuge to cover a fear of failure than a forthright avowal of the artist's independence from societal pressures whenever these threaten to inhibit the free play of his imaginative powers. Tennyson, Browning, and Arnold never went to the lengths of the poets who came after in disassociating themselves from their audience. On the other hand, there is a fundamental error in the prevalent notion that they uncritically shared most of the foibles that, rightly or wrongly, are attributed to the Victorians. Such an opinion overlooks that quality of double awareness. . . .

In their youthful poems Tennyson, Browning, and Arnold revealed the habits of mind, the emotional and intellectual leanings, the kinds of imaginative vision—in other words, the native resources at the disposal of each. Subsequently, from a desire to gain a wide audience for their work and hence to play an influential part in the life of the times, all three poets showed a willingness to make concessions to literary fashions with which they were temperamentally out of sympathy. Resolved, nevertheless, that conformity should involve as little artistic loss as possible, Tennyson, Browning, and Arnold perfected remarkable techniques for sublimating their private insights without materially falsifying the original perceptions at the heart of their creative impulse. The identification of these insights, along with the recognition of their concealed but vivifying action within poems ostensibly concerned with subjects of different and sometimes contradictory import, draws attention to the true centers of poetic intent in Tennyson, Browning, and Arnold, and thus provides a basis for reassessing their total achievement.

Tennyson's Metrical Mastery

T.S. Eliot

T.S. Eliot argues that Tennyson is a great poet
because in his great volume of poems he displays
variety and, more importantly, technical excellence.
Tennyson, Eliot maintains, created lines with metrical and rhythmic beauty and had an ear for finely
tuned speech sounds. Even while Eliot criticizes
Tennyson for his values, dull storytelling, insincere
thoughts, and shallow emotions, he admires him for
the beauty of his poetry. According to Eliot, the best
of Tennyson comes together in *In Memoriam*, a long
elegy that illustrates technical flair while conveying
sincere emotion. T.S. Eliot, an American who became a British citizen, revolutionized modern poetry
with his criticism and his long poem *The Wasteland*.
He is also the author of "The Lovesong of J. Alfred
Prufrock," *Four Quartets*, and the plays *Murder in the
Cathedral* and *The Cocktail Party*.

Tennyson is a great poet, for reasons that are perfectly clear.
He has three qualities which are seldom found together except in the greatest poets: abundance, variety, and complete
competence. We therefore cannot appreciate his work unless
we read a good deal of it. We may not admire his aims: but
whatever he sets out to do, he succeeds in doing, with a mastery which gives us the sense of confidence that is one of the
major pleasures of poetry. His variety of metrical accomplishment is astonishing. Without making the mistake of trying to
write Latin verse in English, he knew everything about Latin
versification that an English poet could use; and he said of
himself that he thought he knew the quantity of the sounds of
every English word except perhaps *scissors*. He had the finest
ear of any English poet since Milton. He was the master of
Swinburne; and the versification of Swinburne, himself a

"In Memoriam," by T.S. Eliot. Reprinted from *Essays Ancient and Modern*, by T.S. Eliot
(London: Faber & Faber, 1936), by permission of Faber & Faber Ltd. and Harcourt
Brace on behalf of the Estate of T.S. Eliot.

classical scholar, is often crude and sometimes cheap, in comparison with Tennyson's. Tennyson extended very widely the range of active metrical forms in English: in *Maud* alone the variety is prodigious. But innovation in metric is not to be measured solely by the width of the deviation from accepted practice. It is a matter of the historical situation: at some moments a more violent change may be necessary than at others. The problem differs at every period. At some times, a violent revolution may be neither possible nor desirable; at such times, a change which may appear very slight, is the change which the important poet will make. The innovation of Pope, after Dryden, may not seem very great; but it is the mark of the master to be able to make small changes which will be highly significant, as at another time to make radical changes, through which poetry will curve back again to its norm.

There is an early poem, only published in the official biography, which already exhibits Tennyson as a master. According to a note, Tennyson later expressed regret that he had removed the poem from his Juvenilia; it is a fragmentary *Hesperides,* in which only the 'Song of the Three Sisters' is complete. The poem illustrates Tennyson's classical learning and his mastery of metre. The first stanza of 'The Song of the Three Sisters' is as follows:

> *The Golden Apple, the Golden Apple, the hallow'd fruit,*
> *Guard it well, guard it warily,*
> *Singing airily,*
> *Standing about the charmed root.*
> *Round about all is mute,*
> *As the snowfield on the mountain peaks,*
> *As the sandfield at the mountain foot.*
> *Crocodiles in briny creeks*
> *Sleep and stir not; all is mute.*
> *If ye sing not, if ye make false measure,*
> *We shall lose eternal pleasure,*
> *Worth eternal want of rest.*
> *Laugh not loudly: watch the treasure*
> *Of the wisdom of the West.*
> *In a corner wisdom whispers. Five and three*
> *(Let it not be preach'd abroad) make an awful mystery:*
> *For the blossom unto threefold music bloweth;*
> *Evermore it is born anew,*
> *And the sap in threefold music floweth,*
> *From the root,*
> *Drawn in the dark,*
> *Up to the fruit,*
> *Creeping under the fragrant bark,*

Liquid gold, honeysweet through and through.
Keen-eyed Sisters, singing airily,
Looking warily
Every way,
Guard the apple night and day,
Lest one from the East come and take it away.

A young man who can write like that has not much to learn
about metric; and the young man who wrote these lines
somewhere between 1828 and 1830 was doing something
new. There is something not derived from any of his predecessors. In some of Tennyson's early verse the influence of
Keats is visible—in songs and in blank verse; and less successfully, there is the influence of Wordsworth, as in *Dora.*
But in the lines I have just quoted, and in the two Mariana
poems, *The Sea-Fairies, The Lotos-Eaters, The Lady of
Shalott* and elsewhere, there is something wholly new.

All day within the dreamy house,
The doors upon their hinges creak'd;
The blue fly sung in the pane; the mouse
Behind the mouldering wainscoat shriek'd,
Or from the crevice peer'd about.

The blue fly sung in the pane (the line would be ruined if
you substituted *sang* for *sung*) is enough to tell us that
something important has happened.

The reading of long poems is not nowadays much prac-
tised: in the age of Tennyson it appears to have been easier.
For a good many long poems were not only written but
widely circulated; and the level was high: even the second-
rate long poems of that time, like *The Light of Asia,* are better worth reading than most long modern novels. But Tennyson's long poems are not long poems in quite the same
sense as those of his contemporaries. They are very different
in kind from *Sordello* or *The Ring and the Book,* to name the
greatest by the greatest of his contemporary poets. *Maud* and
In Memoriam are each a series of poems, given form by the
greatest lyrical resourcefulness that a poet has ever shown.
The Idylls of the King have merits and defects similar to those
of *The Princess.* An *idyll* is a 'short poem descriptive of some
picturesque scene or incident'; in choosing the name Tennyson perhaps showed an appreciation of his limitations. For
his poems are always descriptive, and always picturesque;
they are never really narrative. *The Idylls of the King* are no
different in kind from some of his early poems; the *Morte d'
Arthur* is in fact an early poem. *The Princess* is still an idyll,

but an idyll that is too long. Tennyson's versification in this poem is as masterly as elsewhere: it is a poem which we must read, but which we excuse ourselves from reading twice. And it is worth while recognizing the reason why we return again and again, and are always stirred by the lyrics which intersperse it, and which are among the greatest of all poetry of their kind, and yet avoid the poem itself. It is not, as we may think while reading, the outmoded attitude towards the relations of the sexes, the exasperating views on the subjects of matrimony, celibacy and female education, that make us recoil from *The Princess.** We can swallow the most antipathetic doctrines if we are given an exciting narrative. But for narrative Tennyson had no gift at all. For a static poem, and a moving poem, on the same subject, you have only to compare his *Ulysses* with the condensed and intensely exciting narrative of that hero in the XXVIth Canto of Dante's *Inferno.* Dante is telling a story. Tennyson is only stating an elegiac mood. The very greatest poets set before you real men talking, carry you on in real events moving. Tennyson could not tell a story at all. It is not that in *The Princess* he tries to tell a story and failed: it is rather that an idyll protracted to such length becomes unreadable. So *The Princess* is a dull poem; one of the poems of which we may say, that they are beautiful but dull.

But in *Maud* and in *In Memoriam*, Tennyson is doing what every conscious artist does, turning his limitations to good purpose. Of the content of *Maud*, I cannot think so highly as does Mr. Humbert Wolfe, in his interesting essay on Tennyson which is largely a defence of the supremacy of that poem. For me, *Maud* consists of a few very beautiful lyrics, such as *O let the solid ground, Birds in the high Hall-garden,* and *Go not, happy day,* around which the semblance of a dramatic situation has been constructed with the greatest metrical virtuosity. The whole situation is unreal; the ravings of the lover on the edge of insanity sound false, and fail, as do the bellicose bellowings, to make one's flesh creep with sincerity. It would be foolish to suggest that Tennyson ought to have gone through some experience similar to that described: for a poet with dramatic gifts, a situation quite re-

---

* For a revelation of the Victorian mind on these matters, and of opinions to which Tennyson would probably have subscribed, see the Introduction by Sir Edward Strachey, Bt., to his emasculated edition of the *Morte D'Arthur* of Malory, still current. Sir Edward admired the *Idylls of the King.*

mote from his personal experience may release the strongest emotion. And I do not believe for a moment that Tennyson was a man of mild feelings or weak passions. There is no evidence in his poetry that he knew the experience of violent passion for a woman; but there is plenty of evidence of emotional intensity and violence—but of emotion so deeply suppressed, even from himself, as to tend rather towards the blackest melancholia than towards dramatic action. And it is emotion which, so far as my reading of the poems can discover, attained no ultimate clear purgation. I should reproach Tennyson not for mildness, or tepidity, but rather for lack of serenity.

> *Of love that never found his earthly close,*
> *What sequel?*

The fury of *Maud* is shrill rather than deep, though one feels in every passage what exquisite adaptation of metre to the mood Tennyson is attempting to express. I think that the effect of feeble violence, which the poem as a whole produces, is the result of a fundamental error of form. A poet can express his feelings as fully through a dramatic, as through a lyrical form; but *Maud* is neither one thing nor the other: just as *The Princess* is more than an idyll, and less than a narrative. In *Maud*, Tennyson neither identifies himself with the lover, nor identifies the lover with himself: consequently, the real feelings of Tennyson, profound and tumultuous as they are, never arrive at expression.

It is, in my opinion, in *In Memoriam*, that Tennyson finds full expression. Its technical merit alone is enough to ensure its perpetuity. While Tennyson's technical competence is everywhere masterly and satisfying, *In Memoriam* is the less unapproachable of all his poems. Here are one hundred and thirty-two passages, each of several quatrains in the same form, and never monotony or repetition. And the poem has to be comprehended as a whole. We may not memorize a few passages, we cannot find a 'fair sample'; we have to comprehend the whole of a poem which is essentially the length that it is. We may choose to remember:

> *Dark house, by which once more I stand*
> *Here in the long unlovely street,*
> *Doors, where my heart was used to beat*
> *So quickly, waiting for a hand,*
>
> *A hand that can be clasp'd no more—*
> *Behold me, for I cannot sleep,*

And like a guilty thing I creep
At earliest morning to the door.

He is not here; but far away
The noise of life begins again,
And ghastly thro' the drizzling rain
On the bald street breaks the blank day.

This is great poetry, economical of words, a universal emotion in what could only be an English town: and it gives me the shudder that I fail to get from anything in *Maud*. But such a passage, by itself, is not *In Memoriam: In Memoriam* is the whole poem. It is unique: it is a long poem made by putting together lyrics, which have only the unity and continuity of a diary, the concentrated diary of a man confessing himself. It is a diary of which we have to read every word.

Apparently Tennyson's contemporaries, once they had accepted *In Memoriam*, regarded it as a message of hope and reassurance to their rather fading Christian faith. It happens now and then that a poet by some strange accident expresses the mood of his generation, at the same time that he is expressing a mood of his own which is quite remote from that of his generation. This is not a question of insincerity: there is an amalgam of yielding and opposition below the level of consciousness. Tennyson himself, on the conscious level of the man who talks to reporters and poses for photographers, to judge from remarks made in conversation and recorded in his son's Memoir, consistently asserted a convinced, if somewhat sketchy, Christian belief. And he was a friend of Frederick Denison Maurice—nothing seems odder about that age than the respect which its eminent people felt for each other. Nevertheless, I get a very different impression from *In Memoriam* from that which Tennyson's contemporaries seem to have got. It is of a very much more interesting and tragic Tennyson. His biographers have not failed to remark that he had a good deal of the temperament of the mystic—certainly not at all the mind of the theologian. He was desperately anxious to hold the faith of the believer, without being very clear about what he wanted to believe: he was capable of illumination which he was incapable of understanding. The 'Strong Son of God, immortal Love', with an invocation of whom the poem opens, has only a hazy connexion with the Logos, or the Incarnate God. Tennyson is distressed by the idea of a mechanical universe; he is naturally, in lamenting his friend, teased by the hope of immortality and reunion beyond death. Yet the renewal craved for seems at best but a continuance, or a substitute for the joys of friendship upon earth. His desire for immortality never is quite the desire for Eternal Life; his concern is for the loss of man rather than for the gain of God.

> *shall he,*
> *Man, her last work, who seem'd so fair,*
> *Such splendid purpose in his eyes,*
> *Who roll'd the psalm to wintry skies,*
> *Who built him fanes of fruitless prayer,*
>
> *Who trusted God was love indeed,*
> *And love Creation's final law—*
> *Though Nature, red in tooth and claw*
> *With ravine shriek'd against his creed—*
>
> *Who loved, who suffer'd countless ills.*
> *Who battled for the True, the Just,*
> *Be blown about the desert dust,*
> *Or seal'd within the iron hills?*

That strange abstraction, 'Nature', becomes a real god or goddess, perhaps more real, at moments, to Tennyson than God (*'Are God and Nature then at strife?'*). The hope of immortality is confused (typically of the period) with the hope of the gradual and steady improvement of this world. Much has been said of Tennyson's interest in contemporary science, and of the impression of Darwin. *In Memoriam,* in any case, antedates *The Origin of Species* by several years, and the belief in social progress by democracy antedates it by many more; and I suspect that the faith of Tennyson's age in human progress would have been quite as strong even had the discoveries of Darwin been postponed by fifty years. And after all, there is no logical connexion: the belief in progress being current already, the discoveries of Darwin were harnessed to it:

> *No longer half-akin to brute,*
> *For all we thought, and loved and did*
> *And hoped, and suffer'd, is but seed*
> *Of what in them is flower and fruit;*
>
> *Whereof the man, that with me trod*
> *This planet, was a noble type*
> *Appearing ere the times were ripe,*
> *That friend of mine who lives in God,*
>
> *That God, which ever lives and loves,*
> *One God, one law, one element,*
> *And one far-off divine event,*
> *To which the whole creation moves.*

These lines show an interesting compromise between the religious attitude and, what is quite a different thing, the belief in human perfectibility; but the contrast was not so apparent to Tennyson's contemporaries. They may have been taken in by it, but I don't think that Tennyson himself was, quite: his feelings were more honest than his mind. There is evidence elsewhere—even in an early poem, *Locksley Hall*, for example—that Tennyson by no means regarded with complacency all the changes that were going on about him in the progress of industrialism and the rise of the mercantile and manufacturing and banking classes; and he may have contemplated the future of England, as his years drew out, with increasing gloom. Temperamentally, he was opposed to the doctrine that he was moved to accept and to praise.*

Tennyson's feelings, I have said, were honest; but they were usually a good way below the surface. *In Memoriam* can, I think, justly be called a religious poem, but for another reason than that which made it seem religious to his contemporaries. It is not religious because of the quality of its faith, but because of the quality of its doubt. Its faith is a poor thing, but its doubt is a very intense experience. *In Memoriam* is a poem of despair, but of despair of a religious kind. And to qualify its despair with the adjective 'religious' is to elevate it above most of its derivatives. For *The City of Dreadful Night*, and *Shropshire Lad*, and the poems of Thomas Hardy, are small work in comparison with *In Memoriam*: it is greater than they and comprehends them.**

In ending we must go back to the beginning and remember that *In Memoriam* would not be a great poem, or Tennyson a great poet, without the technical accomplishment. Tennyson is the great master of metric as well as of melancholia; I do not think any poet in English has ever had a finer ear for vowel sound, as well as a subtler feeling for some moods of anguish:

> *Dear as remember'd kisses after death,*
> *And sweet as those by hopeless fancy feign'd*
> *On lips that are for others; deep as love,*
> *Deep as first love, and wild with all regret.*

---

* See, in Harold Nicolson's admirable *Tennyson*, p. 252 ff.
** There are other kinds of despair. Davidson's great poem, *Thirty Bob a Week*, is not derivative from Tennyson. On the other hand, there are other things derivative from Tennyson besides *Atalanta in Calydon*. Compare the poems of William Morris with *The Voyage of Maeldune*, and *Barrack Room Ballads* with several of Tennyson's later poems.

And this technical gift of Tennyson's is no slight thing. Tennyson lived in a time which was already acutely time-conscious: a great many things seemed to be happening, railways were being built, discoveries were being made, the face of the world was changing. That was a time busy in keeping up to date. It had, for the most part, no hold on permanent things, on permanent truths about man and god and life and death. The surface of Tennyson stirred about with his time; and he had nothing to which to hold fast except his unique and unerring feeling for the sounds of words. But in this he had something that no one else had. Tennyson's surface, his technical accomplishment, is intimate with his depths: what we most quickly see about Tennyson is that which moves between the surface and the depths, that which is of slight importance. By looking innocently at the surface we are most likely to come to the depths, to the abyss of sorrow. Tennyson is not only a minor Virgil, he is also with Virgil as Dante saw him, a Virgil among the Shades, the saddest of all English poets, among the Great in Limbo, the most instinctive rebel against the society in which he was the most perfect conformist.

Tennyson seems to have reached the end of his spiritual development with *In Memoriam;* there followed no reconciliation, no resolution.

> *And now no sacred staff shall break in blossom,*
> *No choral salutation lure to light*
> *A spirit sick with perfume and sweet night,*

or rather with twilight, for Tennyson faced neither the darkness nor the light, in his later years. The genius, the technical power, persisted to the end, but the spirit had surrendered. A gloomier end than that of Baudelaire: Tennyson had no *singulier avertissement.* And having turned aside from the journey through the dark night, to become the surface flatterer of his own time, he has been rewarded with the despite of an age that succeeds his own in shallowness.

The Moment of Illumination in Browning's Dramatic Monologues

Shiv K. Kumar

Shiv K. Kumar analyzes the illuminating moment, or epiphany, a difficult element in Robert Browning's dramatic monologues. This moment is a focal point in which the poem expresses such insight, such heightened awareness that a single temporal experience seems to reveal a universal truth. Kumar identifies emotional, aesthetic, and religious moments and discusses poems that illustrate each. Shiv K. Kumar has lectured on British Victorian literature at Osmania University, Hyderabad, India, and at the University of Northern Iowa. He is the author of *Bergson and the Stream of Consciousness Novel* and editor of *British Romantic Poets: Recent Revaluations.*

In one of her earliest letters to Robert Browning, Elizabeth Barrett[1] attempts to categorize his "vision" in terms of the traditional dualism: "You have in your vision two worlds, or to use the language of the schools of the day, you are both subjective and objective in the habits of your mind. You can deal with abstract thought and with human passion in the most passionate sense." Indeed, Browning often does indulge in explicit statements, or what [critic Hoxie] Fairchild calls his "giveaways," and he sometimes seems to oscillate between the rational and the intuitive. . . . He is constantly attempting to penetrate the vital core of *Existenz*, not intellectually, but intuitively "in the most passionate sense," shorn of all metaphysical trappings. This kernel of experi-

---

1. Elizabeth Barrett, a British poet, was married to Robert Browning in 1846.

ence, Browning feels, manifests itself not in the grey "dailiness" of life, but in certain dramatic moments of heightened perception when a seemingly trivial experience becomes charged with fresh significance.

THE MEANING OF BROWNING'S "MOMENTS"

It seems that Browning's *modus operandi*[2] is to capture such moments of illumination. In a letter to Elizabeth Barrett, he remarks: ". . . that is a way of mine which you must have observed; that foolish concentrating of thought and feeling, *for a moment,* on some one little spot of a character or anything else indeed, and in the attempt to do justice and develop whatever may seem ordinarily to be overlooked in it,—that over-vehement *insisting* on, and giving an undue prominence to, the same—which has the effect of taking away from the importance of the rest of the related objects which, in truth, are not considered at all . . ." But it is in another letter to Elizabeth Barrett that he uses the metaphor of *phare*[3] to emphasize momentariness as the prime basis of his poetic experience. Here he describes his poems as "very escapes of my inner power, which lives in me like the light in those crazy Mediterranean phares I have watched at sea, wherein the light is ever revolving in a dark gallery, bright and alive, and only after a weary interval leaps out, *for a moment,* from the narrow chink, and then goes on with the blind wall between it and you." And again, in a letter to [a friend] Julia Wedgwood, he refers to his poetic concept of instantaneous illuminations, those "rare flashes of momentary conviction that come and go in the habitual dusk and doubt of life.". . .

Before we undertake to assess the multifaceted significance of the moment, appearing in the dramatic monologues of Robert Browning under such protean guises as the moment *naked, terrible, fateful, burning, warm, mighty, rapturous, blessed, eternal* (indeed, he seems to have run through the entire gamut of adjectives suggesting the intense quality of such moments), it is imperative to define its most distinctive characteristic. . . . The protagonist in each of his dramatic monologues is not a mere entity in an abstract Hegelian process, but an individual caught existentially in a state of tension which, according to [philosopher Soren] Kierkegaard, is "the frontier between time and eternity." At

2. method of operation   3. lighthouse; beacon

the point where the present moment encounters eternity, and is transformed into the eternal "now," the individual perceives a fresh meaning in life; he is transformed into a new existence; he realizes thereafter his peculiar relation to his environment. It is the function of a poet to symbolize this intersection between time and eternity; as Browning observes in a letter to [British essayist John] Ruskin, all poetry is fundamentally concerned with the problem of "putting the infinite within the finite.". . . Meaningful existence, therefore, is not merely quantitative, but qualitative in essence; it recognizes the paradox of infinity in the finite, and eternal Being in temporal Becoming.

Let us now examine how the moment in Browning's dramatic monologues manifests itself on the emotional, aesthetic and religious planes, respectively.

On the emotional plane, Browning holds up for closer scrutiny the moment of greatest intensity between man and woman, when nothing distracts the heart from participating fully in the experience of love. He selects from the stream of diurnal routine certain luminous moments in which the lover realizes his true identity in relationship to his beloved. Eternity congeals itself in that instant, and conversely the moment acquires cumulatively the vitality of eternity. This nature of "the moment eternal" Browning describes in a lyric of exquisite beauty entitled "Now." Here the lover is so deeply absorbed in the ecstatic moment that, unconcerned as to "how long such suspension may linger," he tries to achieve complete identification, however transient, with his beloved. All that he asks is a moment of complete affirmation, so that they both may "condense,/ In a rapture of rage, for perfection's endowment,/ Thought and feeling and soul and sense—/ Merged in a moment . . ." It is significant to note here that Browning considers it essential for the lover to bring his entire being to bear on such a consummation, for in "ecstasy's utmost we clutch at the core.". . .

On the aesthetic plane, Browning's theory of art—of music, painting and poetic creation—also recognizes the ecstatic moment as a point in perception when the object reveals itself in its entirety from the inside; it is seen and felt rather than remembered and categorized. In the process of creative incubation, when the secondary imagination is at work, the artist is suddenly caught up in the "naked moment," like an excalibur thrust out of water, and all the disparate strands of thought and feeling merge esemplastically[4] into a harmonious pattern. His vision, hitherto partial, casual and fragmentary, achieves its totality and all "the broken arcs" melt into "a perfect round"; all multiplicity is unified.

Abt Vogler, one of Browning's most dynamic monologues, is a typical example of his treatment of the moment. Abt Vogler has been "extemporizing upon the musical instrument of his invention," symbolizing the free play of the mind. Uninhibited by any written score, he is conjuring up notes "fresh from the Protoplast," his "manifold music" resisting the imposition of any "structure," when suddenly "a flash of the will that can," makes him exclaim, "But here is the finger of God!". . .

The painters in Browning's dramatic monologues are equally concerned with capturing such moments when, to quote Pictor Ignotus, the artist is "straight like thunder, sunk to the center, of an instant." From the continuum of the life-flow, the painter, in a moment of heightened perception, apprehends the potential of a seemingly trivial gesture, motion or glance. Fra Lippo Lippi, for instance, describes how he waits for a momentary vision of "the breathless fellow at the altar-foot, fresh from the murder," "the proper twinkle in your eye," or "your cullion's hanging face.". . .

Though the Duke of Ferrara is not a painter, his susceptibilities are markedly aesthetic; in fact, he prefers to be amply compensated by Fra Pandolf's portrait of his wife rather than live with a young woman whose "looks went everywhere." His appreciation of "that piece a wonder," "the depth and passion of its earnest glance," "the faint/Half-flush that dies along her throat,"—shows the sensitive perception of a seasoned connoisseur of art. So in murdering his wife and zealously preserving her portrait, he has salvaged what he considers to be the kernel and thrown the husk away. The image of the duke himself, as it emerges from *My Last Duchess*, is subtly complex, wrapped in subterfuges and innuendoes. What, then, is his basic motivation? He reveals his innermost soul, not in analyzing overtly his motive, but in making a casual observation about his bronze statue. As he invites the Count's envoy to "meet the company below," he pauses for a moment on the steps in front of the statue:

4. in the manner of forming or developing into

Notice Neptune, though,
Taming a sea-horse, thought a rarity,
Which Claus of Innsbruck cast in bronze for me!

Here in a casual aside is crystallized for the reader the duke in his full amplitude—a man charged with overwhelming possessiveness, uncompromising egotism and self-complacency, who must bend everything to his inviolate will.

On the plane of religious experience, the moment, in some of Browning's dramatic monologues, symbolizes the incarnation, God's revelation as the Christ, through His infinite love and compassion for man. Cosmic experience, otherwise a remote concept of man's relation to the infinite, now concretizes itself in the shape of the Christ. . . .

It is unnecessary to trace any direct theological or philosophical influences on Browning's mind. Was he, for instance, influenced by the epiphany feast?[5] Or did he get the idea from the pagan festivals associated with the Dionysiac cult, at which the god appeared momentarily (the "epiphany" of Dionysus[6]) as his frenzied worshippers burst into *ekstasis*,[7] only to disappear soon into another world? If some of his poems are epiphanic in overtones, it is probably because Browning was guided more by his poetic sensitivity than by any formal ritual or dogma.

Browning's so-called religious poems, which center around the themes of revelation and the incarnation, fall into two distinct categories; firstly, those poems in which the main character's mental processes persistently follow a predetermined course until he achieves the final illumination, and, secondly, those poems in which the epiphanic revelation explodes upon the mind, "as if in a thunder peal." Although both kinds of religious experience ultimately culminate in sudden spiritual enlightenment, it is obvious that the involuntary or unpremeditated mode of dramatic perception comes closer to Browning's innate sensibilities. In Bergsonian terminology,[8] these two varieties of religious experience are like two distinct planes of mental tension: one on which the mind deliberately summons up images from the past and is thus involved in a process of *mémoire volontaire,* and the other plane on which remembrances flow into the mind in-

<hr>

5. a Christian feast celebrating the manifestation of the divine nature of Jesus as represented by the Magi; celebrated on January 6   6. the Greek god of wine   7. intense joy or delight; emotion that carries one beyond rational thought and self-control   8. from French philosopher Henri Bergson

tuitively and involuntarily signifying *mémoire par excellence.*

Let us first consider those poems in which revelation comes as a sequel to premeditation. Take, for instance, *Christmas Eve* in which the soliloquist depicts himself in a Florentine church, on a particular Christmas eve, reflecting on the utter inadequacy of the purely formal and soulless modes of worship ("the pig-of-lead like pressure/ of the preaching man's immense stupidity/ As he poured his doctrine forth"). As he walks away from the congregation, and finds himself alone on the hillside, "suddenly/ The rain and the wind ceased." He senses the presence of Christ.

> All at once I looked up with terror.
> He was there.
> He himself with his human air,
> On the narrow pathway, just before.
> I saw the back of him, no more . . .

In that "rapturous moment," he sees the Heavenly vision; he reaches for "the flying robe"; he then realizes

> We are made in his image, to witness him . . .
> No mere exposition of morality
> Made or in part or in totality
> Should win you to give it worship . . .

. . . In *An Epistle,* the Arab Physician's twenty-second let-

---

"Now"

Browning's poem "Now" seems to compress time, space, and all elements of the human psyche into a momentary meeting of a couple's love.

Out of your whole life give but a moment!
All of your life that has gone before,
All to come after it,—so you ignore,
So you make perfect the present,—condense,
In a rapture of rage, for perfection's endowment,
Thought and feeling and soul and sense—
Merged in a moment which gives me at last
You around me for once, you beneath me, above me—
Me—sure that despite of time future, time past,—
This tick of our life-time's one moment you love me!
How long such suspension may linger? Ah, Sweet—
The moment eternal—just that and no more—
When ecstasy's utmost we clutch at the core
While cheeks burn, arms open, eyes shut and lips meet!

Robert Browning, "Now," 1889.

ter to his master Abib, the former experiences the dramatic moment of affirmation without the least possible premeditation. Written in a fluid and colloquial style, following the lines and curves of his thoughts, the poem depicts him suddenly confronted by a unique phenomenon, which his scientific mind cannot comprehend. Both Lazarus's resurrection, and his transformation into new dimensions of perception, are beyond the limited compass of "this picker of learning's crumbs." Not equipped to understand the depth and complexity of an experience transcending both life and death, Karshish refers to it as a mere triviality "to avoid the stuffing of my travelscript." But "The Man had something in the look of him—/ His case has struck me far more than 'tis worth." He rambles on in his perplexity, when suddenly in an ecstatic moment of dramatic affirmation, he senses the authenticity of the miracle. His analytical perspective can no longer ignore the power and the glory of the Christ, the self-giving Love:

> The very God! think, Abib; dost thou think?
> So, the All-Great, were the All-Loving too—
> So, through the thunder comes a human voice
> Saying, "O heart I made, a heart beats here!
> "Face, my hands fashioned, see it myself!
> "Thou hast no power nor mayst conceive of mine,
> "But love I gave thee, with myself to love,
> "And thou must love me who have died for thee!

Although *Cristina* is essentially a love lyric, in it Browning also plumbs the depths of true religious experience. Here he suggests that a life completely devoid of any moments of illumination would be dark, mute, almost evil. It is Satan's prime objective to keep man wrapped up in routine responses, his mind chained in rational self-complacency. But

> Oh, we're sunk enough here, God knows!
> But not quite so sunk that moments,
> Sure tho' seldom, are denied us . . .

Indeed, these "flashes struck from midnights," these "fire-flames that noondays kindle," are God's mysterious signs by which the eternal breaks into the temporal that man may "catch God's secret," and earth may commune with heaven.

The Search for Self-Knowledge in Arnold's Poetry

Allan Brick

Allan Brick identifies Matthew Arnold's view regarding his search for self-knowledge: Arnold says that self-knowledge is attainable only at a point of balance between active involvement in the world and withdrawal from it, a position impossible for humans to sustain. Brick shows how this theme recurs in poem after poem and explains that Arnold's narrators or protagonists who persist in the search ultimately withdraw and die. According to Brick, Arnold concludes that it is arrogant even to embark on the search. Allan Brick, a scholar of Victorian poets, has contributed to literary journals specializing in Victorian literature.

[Matthew] Arnold insists that there is an objective reality over which man's will has no control—an amoral Nature which is not man's friend nor his foe nor in any way cognizant of him, and which subjects him to the rules of change and death. While recognizing that it is natural for man to persist in the illusion that he can understand or even contain "reality," Arnold reveals a world thoroughly independent of the "dreams" which constitute human consciousness. . . .

For Arnold the discovery of reality is the discovery of self *vis à vis*[1] the outer world; it comes at a point of equilibrium between, on the one hand, engagement in society, in love, in ideals and, on the other, isolation from action, from passion, from principle, indeed, from life itself. Neither the self nor the outer world are noumena[2] which can be seen into or, ex-

1. in relation to   2. objects that can be intuited only by the intellect and not perceived by the senses

Excerpted from Allan Brick, "Equilibrium in the Poetry of Matthew Arnold," *University of Toronto Quarterly*, October 1960. Reprinted by permission of the publisher, the University of Toronto Press. Copyright ©1960 by the University of Toronto Press.

cept in the most limited and exterior manner, understood; and this fact can force man either to accept oversimplified forms (illusions) in place of reality, or to despair of imposing upon complex existence any forms whatsoever. At a point of equilibrium man must develop the humility and the strength to "hold his rudder fast" against winds that would blow him to either side.

"MYCERINUS, THE SICK KING OF BOKHARA"

King Mycerinus,[3] with only six years to live, decides his notions of religion and justice are illusory forms, "mere phantoms of man's self-tormenting heart," and abandons them, along with the entire context of social existence, to find what meagre reality he can in "the silence of the groves and woods." His withdrawal is to be neither a retirement nor an escape, but a modest affirmation. In the woods, however, he enters upon an endless cycle of satiation and desire, thus replacing the illusions of social activism and religious belief with those of hedonist indulgence. There, as before, he discovers that every perceived phenomenon, every presumed reality, disappears precisely at the instant of possession— that every "feast" insofar as it occurs is gone, leaving no sustaining after taste. It is at this point that Mycerinus, having learned the full lesson about idealist participation, might be imagined to feel the need for a more ultimate withdrawal.

> It may be that sometimes his wondering soul
> From the loud joyful laughter of his lips
> Might shrink half startled, like a guilty man
> Who wrestles with a dream; as some pale shape
> Gliding half hidden through the dusky stems,
> Would thrust a hand before the lifted bowl,
> Whispering: *A little space, and thou art mine!*

Thus "it may be" that there is no ultimate withdrawal save death, and that the King does well to continue in sensual indulgence, struggling to confine beneath smooth brow and clear laugh his fear of that sole reality. Or "it may be" that for the brief interval before death, even as the feasting continues, Mycerinus pauses inwardly to "take measure of his soul," and is thereby "calm'd, ennobled, comforted, sustain'd." In the darkness, peering at the noumenon of self, the poet cannot assert anything definite. All he can do is chronicle from a distance Mycerinus' problem, and speculate on

---

3. protagonist in "Mycerinus, the Sick King of Bokhara"

the existence of a solution. The poem ends in mystery, as Arnold represents the impossibility of narrator and audience ever discovering anything about noumenal Mycerinus—the impossibility of the ego ever discovering anything essential about itself and what surrounds it:

> And when the mirth wax'd loudest, with dull sound
> Sometimes from the grove's centre echoes came,
> To tell his wondering people of their king;
> In the still night, across the steaming flats,
> Mix'd with the murmur of the moving Nile.

SAPPHO AND ISEULT

Mycerinus' inward projection of withdrawal itself provides the point of view in "A Modern Sappho."[4] The narrator, Sappho, personifies that subject ego which struggles to hold fast the rudder, now against the force of participation and later against the force of death. At the moment the force of participation, her lover, dominates the entire ego; Sappho (helpless at the helm, as it were) must sit resolutely longing for the proper balance. The lover, like "a republican friend," and like Mycerinus engaged in fleeting pleasures, is now impassioned over the world of illusion: the young and sensuous other woman. Sappho, in torture, awaits the day when time will conquer this love, allowing her hero to be drawn to her. Then, dominating, she may effect for the entire ego an interval of essential equilibrium between the passion of life and the dissolution of death. The torturing mystery lies in the question whether or not such an interval can exist; can there be before death *any* life other than that of a sensual, passionate, self-deluded lover? For it is possible that her very longing is in its violence an uncontrollable impulse toward death, and that the supposed point of balance, once reached, cannot be held:

> —Let my turn, if it *will* come, be swift in arriving!
> Ah! hope cannot long lighten torments like these.
> Hast thou yet dealt him, O life, thy full measure?
> World, have they children yet bow'd at his knee?
> Hast thou with myrtle-leaf crown'd him, O pleasure?
> —Crown, crown him quickly, and leave him for me!

This theme is treated more profoundly in "Tristram and Iseult," for which "A Modern Sappho" may have been a preliminary sketch. Here Tristram symbolizes the participative

---

4. Sappho was a Greek lyric poet from about 600 B.C., a great female lyric poet.

ego. He is involved with two Iseults, neither of whom can fully receive his love—Iseult of Ireland can't because of her separation from him as wife of King Marc, and Iseult of Brittany can't because Tristram is blinded to her by his love for Iseult of Ireland. The first two parts of the poem tell of Tristram's sickness from his love for the unattainable Iseult of Ireland; he dies blinded by the "flooding moonlight" of her beauty. In this portion of the poem Iseult of Brittany is mentioned repeatedly in Tristram's love ravings, but only as the Iseult he does *not* want, despite her admitted purity and goodness. Part Three is devoted to Iseult of Brittany, who, having loved the living Tristram in vain, now survives him. Before, her presence in the poem was covert, but now it is clear that she has been the implicit centre for the poet's sympathy. She is revealed as precisely that inward projection of withdrawal personified by Sappho. Thus the story Iseult tells the children at the end of the poem is the wish fulfillment of Sappho's plea that "life" and the "world" "Crown, crown him quickly, and leave him for me!" Iseult envisions herself as Vivian contriving to cast a spell on the old, but still passionate, magician Merlin, and trapping him fast within her "daisied circle."

The longings of Sappho and Iseult of Brittany represent an inward pull toward stoical control without which the "lover," drawing away into "life" and the "world," would dash himself to pieces—as, indeed, Tristram does. But this pull toward control may result not simply in the inhibition but also in the destruction of the participating self, may effect a virtual suicide. The question is how much force the withdrawing self must exercise in order to restrain the idealist who would be ruthless destroyer of the total ego. Undercurrent, therefore, to the controlled equilibrium envisioned by Sappho and Iseult-Vivian, is the threat of the loved hero's imprisonment or even murder by the *femme fatale*.[5]

SUICIDE AS WITHDRAWAL

The suicide in its most basic form is evident in "The Sick King in Bokhara." Identifying a part of himself with a man who seeks the punishment of death for such sins as are common to all humanity, the King rules: "if he seek to fly,

---

5. a woman of great seductive charm who leads men into compromising or dangerous situations

give way, /Hinder him not, but let him go"; then the King
"softly" casts the first stone, as the sinner, looking up at him
with joy, stays to embrace his execution. The King makes
the extraordinary command that the corpse be brought to
him; but his Vizier,[6] at a loss to understand such sympathy
for strangers, reminds him of the dignity of kingship, and of
the law commanding that such a man be stoned "even were
he thine own mother's son." In thus counselling the King,
the Vizier perceives that the executed sinner is in a sense the
King himself, that the King is similarly human. The King's
sickness is his inability to escape from exactly that awareness; if he could harken to the Vizier and thus stoically ignore his disease of humanity, he could have health, release
from tension. The King struggles to hold a balance between
the sinner who succumbed to his thirsts and the Vizier who,
being old, need not contend with any desire. If all three represent divisions of the human spirit, the final stanzas epitomize the proper action of the will in holding a firm balance
between the cold indifference of reason and the consuming
life of passion. The King concludes, "What I would, I cannot
do," but "what I can do, that I will":

> I have a fretted brick-work tomb
> Upon a hill on the right hand,
> Hard by a close of apricots,
> Upon the road of Samarcand;
>
> Thither, O Vizier, will I bear
> This man my pity could not save,
> And, plucking up the marble flags,
> There lay his body in my grave.
>
> Bring water, nard, and linen rolls!
> Wash off all blood, set smooth each limb!
> Then say: 'He was not wholly vile,
> Because a king shall bury him.'

A similar "suicide"—the killing, or at least abandonment,
of the social self by the withdrawing self—is effected by the
wine of "The World and the Quietist," by "The Strayed Rev-
eller," and by the self-imposed estrangement, the bohemi-
anism, of "The Forsaken Merman" and "The Neckan." "The
Scholar Gypsy" seems to achieve an equilibrium by abandoning his participating self; and yet, insofar as he retreats
from society, the question arises does he, did he ever, exist at
all? Arnold's most profound treatment of this theme is

6. a high officer in Moslem government

"Empedocles on Etna." It is a mistake to read this poem simply as a direct comment on Arnold's age.

"EMPEDOCLES ON ETNA"

"Empedocles" is no Victorian "Wasteland"—no bitter lament over the death of idealism, the impossibility of holding absolute values in this withering modern age—rather it is Arnold's interpretation of the tragedy implicit in human existence in every age. Society will always banish, or at least estrange, its just ruler, and, more important, the just ruler will always find it necessary to withdraw from society; insofar as he is honest and courageous he will destroy his activist self, obliterating the pretension and arrogance of idealism. As Arnold said to [Arthur] Clough, Empedocles says, "Know thyself," but in that very assertion inveighs against the Emersonian idealism which defines the inner self as part and parcel of all things:

> No eye could be too sound
> To observe a world so vast,
> No patience too profound
> To sort what's here amass'd;
> How man may here best live no care too great to explore.

> But we—as some rude guest
> Would change, where'er he roam,
> The manners there profess'd
> To those he brings from home—
> We mark not the world's course, but would have *it* take *ours.*

As all human knowledge is pretentious, so is human "pleasure":

> Pleasure, to our hot grasp,
> Gives flowers after flowers;
> With passionate warmth we clasp
> Hand after hand in ours;
> Now do we soon perceive how fast our youth is spent.

> At once our eyes grow clear!
> We see, in blank dismay,
> Year posting after year,
> Sense after sense decay;
> Our shivering heart is mined by secret discontent.

Thus Arnold spurns all idealism—hedonism as well as religion. He seems to end Act One of "Empedocles" with a direct attack upon Tennysonian idealism, asking, must we

> . . . feign a bliss
> Of doubtful future date,

And, while we dream on this,
Lose all our present state,
And relegate to worlds yet distant our repose?

In Act Two of "Empedocles" Arnold deals with the paradox that life in its most essential form may be death, that indeed there may be no equilibrium possible between participation and utter dissolution. As in "A Modern Sappho," he suggests that release from tension comes only with the annihilation of the participant self, and results in nothing less than the eternal loss of personality. On the volcano's summit Empedocles is poised between the longing for participation and the longing for death. Down the mountainside is his life of participation in the world of men, who will "help him unbend his too tense thought" "till the absence from himself/. . . grow unbearable" and he must again come up here to solitude. But,

. . . he will find its air too keen for him,
And so change back; and many thousand times
Be miserably bandied to and fro
Like a sea-wave, betwixt the world and thee,
Thou young, implacable God! and only death
Can cut his oscillations short, and so
Bring him to poise. There is no other way.

IDEAL KNOWLEDGE UNATTAINABLE

Looking back on such an existence, Empedocles can no longer see any reason to struggle for balance; indeed, to do so may also be an arrogant assertion of idealism. How can he, a prisoner of consciousness, who sees only through its "forms, and modes, and stifling veils," know he is not deluding himself in assuming the possibility of balance. And yet, we might ask, how can he know he is any *less* deluded in believing he can eternalize his "dwindling faculty of joy," can achieve some ultimate equilibrium by precipitate reunion with the elements? Actually we are left in complete doubt, as is Empedocles; for even as he plunges he feels that his belief in finding a life of eternal repose among the elements was but "for a moment." What seems a puzzling blank—a failure in the conception of "Empedocles"—is, rather, its necessary conclusion. We are left with an absolute question: whether Empedocles' joining with the elements is a transcendentalist assertion (and thus itself a valid idealism), as Empedocles hopes it is, or is instead an act of nihilistic futility. The answer cannot be determined, man cannot know that much about himself *vis à vis* outer reality. . . .

For Arnold, the end of poetry is communication not of the idealist power that fuses [Tennyson's protagonists] Saul and Hallam with the resurrected Christ, but of the necessary futility of activism braving an alien reality. Although he emphasizes a search for self-knowledge, a withdrawal from social unreality, this is not the continuing process which for Tennyson, Browning, and their romantic predecessors becomes itself the ultimate truth. In the end Arnold permits nothing but the question: what is man, even to believe he can make such a search?

CHAPTER 4

The Novelists

Victorian
Literature

Five Major Victorian Novelists

Richard Church

Richard Church combines historical information about five novelists with his critical opinions about their works. He identifies Dickens as the era's shining star, praising his characters, his craftsmanship, and his humor. William Thackeray and Anthony Trollope, he says, recorded Victorian traditions of daily life with a calm realism. Charlotte Brontë introduced passion into the Victorian novel, and Emily Brontë's *Wuthering Heights* has a wild fury that places this novel in a category of its own. Richard Church spent part of his career as a civil servant and devoted another part to literary societies. He wrote poetry and fiction and the critical work *British Authors.*

The difficulty about [the Victorian period] in the history of the English novel is that this sudden constellation of major writers creates a fire in the sky and dims the light of the myriad smaller novelists who moved forward at the need of the expanding population, catering for the growing literacy through the agency of the lending libraries, pouring out a stream of fiction, good, bad, and indifferent, a flood whose power was in its mass. . . . Out of this wholeness, as from a mirror, they reflect the world around them, but giving it a warp, a bias, which their genius persuades us to accept, because of its paradoxical presentation of truth. But the truth is *within that particular novelist's own equation.* . . .

CHARLES DICKENS

Of all novelists who have ever made a world of their own, and peopled it, Dickens is the most obvious. He began to write at a time when realism might have become a dominant, rising with the changes in society and glossing them

Excerpted from Richard Church, *The Growth of the English Novel* (London: Methuen, 1951). Reprinted by permission of Laurence Pollinger Ltd. on behalf of the Estate of Richard Church.

with a criticism that would have been an irrefutable accusation. Its work as a method had already begun. But Dickens came and swept it all aside. Yet in his own way he made the criticism of society, and attacked the problems of the writhing industrialism which in its birth-pangs was contorting the whole fabric of Europe, and particularly of England. No novelist has had more direct influence as a reformer of certain abuses in public life. In all his instincts he was democratic; and he worked through instinct rather than through reason. His lower middle-class origin, his acquaintance with near-poverty, his passionate devotion to the *idea* of home-life, his idealization of woman and children, his sentimental streaks crossed with blatant vulgarity (especially in his moments of happiness); in all these aspects he reflected instantly and closely the characteristics of the new democracy which was breeding so rapidly. Yet he contrived to give it roots in an older English social order, so that we recognize a kind of cousinship between his famous characters and those of [Henry] Fielding and [William] Shakespeare. . . .

He splashed his prose about like lime-wash, often in the most crude and garish colours. But here again the contradiction recurs, for in that violent method, he could present centres of stillness where eternity was revealed, lucid and firm, as in the character of Agnes in *David Copperfield.* This statement will aggravate many critics, for it is the fashion to deride Agnes as a prig. But Dickens is impervious to fashions, as he is impervious to good taste. He can make us blush for shame, he can make us angry as we weep at his melodrama, he can work up huge explosions of anger over social problems that he judges only from isolated hardships. But even so he makes us love him and his hundreds of creatures. For to hate Sykes, Fagin, Uriah Heep, Scrooge, and all the other villains, freaks, and misfits who whine and roar their way through his books, is really to love them, because they are tangible, they take us by the heart, and enlarge our acquaintance not only with humanity as it is, but as it might become if life should but take another slant.

Where is the critic to begin a consideration of the Dickens people? Is Pickwick the most representative, because he has sat down in almost every household in Europe and the New World? But if we make that claim, we at once hear Sam Weller shout from the kitchen, boot-brush in hand, or see Peggotty look up from her darning, or Aunt Betsy Trotwood's bucket ear-rings beginning to tremble with indignation. The riches are overwhelming. All that we can do is to acknowledge that Dickens stands at the head of all our novelists, in spite of what the higher critics may say, and in spite too of our own personal reservations. . . .

The critical estimate of Dickens's genius, his craftsmanship, and his contribution to and influence upon the English novel, are still unapproached. But their very elusiveness is part of their nature. We take it for granted in all considerations of the English novel, that Dickens is the most fecund, the most strange and original, yet the most familiar. The terror in the man, the warped and highly-strung intensity, carry his fundamental sanity and good nature, his enormous gift of overflowing humour; and there, in all his contradictions, he stands for ever.

WILLIAM MAKEPEACE THACKERAY

In comparison, William Makepeace Thackeray (1811–63) is a figure in the flat, serene and peaceful. His great popularity has shrunk, and a new generation of readers, whose acquaintance is limited to *Vanity Fair* (1846–48) and *Esmond* (1852), may be unaware that his life was by no means a happy one, beginning with professional uncertainty, a confusion of purposes and false starts, to be followed by the loss of his private fortune and the insanity of his wife after the birth of two daughters. After an affluent childhood and youth, to have to live on the brink of the precipice is even worse than to start from poverty, as Dickens started, for the softly nurtured character is prone to take the frosts of fortune badly. Thackeray never complained, however, but set about to make his living as a journalist after abandoning the idea of becoming a cartoonist. His first books were not successful, for the public could make nothing of them. They hovered between a slightly facetious satire, concerned with class distinctions, and the spirit of realism which was soon to become his genius and make him so important a figure in the development of the English novel.

A Shabby Genteel Story (1839) is an example of his early form; a rambling semi-tale which seems, in retrospect, to be concerned largely with basement kitchens, seamstresses struggling with underpay and overwork . . . , and powdered footmen; a depressing book. With *Barry Lyndon* (1843) he began to find himself, a self that had been set in the upper middle-class of Victorian England. . . .

He was not, like Dickens, driven by a demon. In fact, he made efforts from time to time to find an official job which would lead to his escape from the writer's itch. Fortunately, he was not successful, for had he obtained the position in the Post Office, for which he applied, it is certain that he would not have augmented his job, as did [Anthony] Trollope, by three hours' steady literary work every morning before going to the office.

But the need for such lobbying in Government offices disappeared with the publication of *Vanity Fair* (1846–48). It was instantly successful, and made Thackeray a figure in the literary world of a stature comparable to that of Dickens. He was made first Editor of the new *Cornhill Magazine*, in which Trollope found fame. Thackeray's efforts at writing serial tales for the *Cornhill* were disappointing, but he made up for it by his regular provision of garrulous essays under the title of *Roundabout Papers* (a most characteristic one!). This habit of meandering, of taking the reader into his confidence about the work in hand, was at times maddening; more so today, since the discipline of technique in the art of the novel has been so much tightened up, to the exclusion of the face and form of the author. This legato continuity of mood, half reminiscent, joined Thackeray's novels one with another, giving him scope to indulge his preoccupation with the structure of family life. The marriages, the descendants and antecedents, the cousinships first, second, and third, link his characters, carrying them from book to book, until the reader can hardly see the wood for the family trees. This device makes him, in the long run, an author to whom one becomes addicted, as within a closed society. His clubbability is enormous, and the tendency is to forget, as he himself forgot, that there is a vast mass of human life outside this charmed circle, people of the 'lower orders' (we have nowadays to put the phrase in inverted commas), whose drama we may either ignore or treat with amused condescension. Thackeray was never aware of the danger, or the wickedness, of this attitude, for he represented a class that lived upon artificial assumptions, and wore blinkers which Dickens made it his job to strip off. Within that almost family circle, however, Thackeray had deployed in *Vanity Fair* a contemporary realism, further to be developed in *Pendennis* (1848–50) and *The Newcomes* (1855), which set the mode of fiction in general from that time onwards to the present day.

In *Vanity Fair* this realism is applied to the historical method. But it showed its approach by avoiding the heroic figures and moments. Thackeray rightly called his great book (surely one of the most important novels, from every point of view, in our language) a 'novel without a hero'. Thus the muse of history is similarly treated. We are not shown the field of Waterloo, but the perturbations of social life in Brussels during the weeks preceding the battle: the preliminaries in London, in the political and financial worlds, or at least in the houses of their women-folk in Belgravia. For the second time in fiction, we find an author accepting the world as he found it, Thackeray going direct to Fielding for the formula, or rather the decision to have no formula. With a lofty ethical standard, he refused to allow any of his characters to be embodiments of that standard. Their efforts to conform to it, to pretend to it, to avoid it, are what interested him, and he pictured them in all their resolutions and failings, wart by wart, but without the violence of caricature or the distortion of satire. Here were human beings as we know them, the gentle and dull Amelia, the tricky, vain, charming Becky Sharp. Even the villain of the piece, Lord Steyne, was true to life. Indeed, he was painted from life, the model being the old Regency buck the Marquis of Hertford. Over all this vast concourse of mortals, for Thackeray's stage, like his life, was always crowded; and over all the rich scene painting, there flows the almost engulfing prose whose style is so marked. Today, it is somewhat too button-holing and familiar for our taste. . . .

ANTHONY TROLLOPE

Anthony Trollope (1815–82) may be called a disciple of Thackeray exploiting what Henry James called 'a genius for the usual'. Second thoughts about him reveal qualities that recall not a little the conciseness of texture of Jane Austen, the determination of characters within a prescribed field, the avoidance of abstract problems, philosophical grandeurs, poetic afflatus. He knew much more about the world of affairs than Jane Austen, for he was an administrative official in the Post Office, and moved about the British Isles freely in the pursuit of his duties. Further, his childhood had been harassed by family troubles, for his father was a barrister of odd temper and bad health, a failure in his profession, and doomed to be kept and nursed by his wife, an indomitable woman who for this purpose took to writing at the age of fifty-five and made a successful career, turning out over a hundred books before she laid down her pen, and at the same time bringing up, in England and later in Belgium, her several children. This story is told vividly in Trollope's *Autobiography*, a characteristic piece of work that shows the vigour, the downright honesty, the capable and patient integrity (somewhat lacking in fantasy and charm) which tincture the objective scene of his novels.

Trollope was nineteen when he entered the Civil Service. He took the work seriously, and not as a sinecure.[1] It was he who introduced the pillar-box for posting letters, now a world-wide feature of civilization. Every day before going to work he got up at six o'clock and wrote for three hours, at the rate of a thousand words an hour, timed by his watch on the desk before him. After finishing one three-decker, he began another the next morning. This admirable professional address to the art of letters produced a huge body of fiction, some of it pedestrian and dull, most of it on a level that has kept it above the flood of oblivion. His best books, the Barsetshire series, begin with *The Warden* (1855), his nearest approach to poetic atmosphere, and continue with *Barchester Towers* (1857), *Dr Thorne* (1858), *Framley Parsonage* (1861), *The Small House at Allington* (1864), and the *Last Chronicle of Barset* (1867). These books brought him success after the failure of several with an Irish setting. . . .

The publication of the *Autobiography* in 1883, at the height of his popularity, did Trollope an ill-service, thereby showing once again that he never fully concealed a certain naïvety and lack of worldly self-interest. In the eighties, the 'Grosvenor Gallery, greenery-yallery'[2] fashion had set in, with [playwright] Oscar Wilde walking down Piccadilly [Street] with a lily in his hand. [Writer] Walter Pater was the deity of the moment, and it was thought *de rigueur*[3] to write like him, every sentence revised a dozen times, in the search for the immaculate word. Here came Trollope confessing that he worked like a bricklayer, so many bricks a day, then down tools! It was an insult to literature, just as in our time it has been an insult to write poetry that is instantly intelligible and unadorned with a dozen or so concealed quotations from and allusions to forgotten minor writers of the past, and pendant with tags in several other tongues than English.

Trollope punched a hole right through his own fame. Not until between the two World Wars was he rediscovered, and found to be a major novelist of distinctive flavour and a massive sagacity.

His value as a factor in the historical and aesthetic development of the English novel is that he walks solidly (one can hear his footfall) down the middle of the road of tradition. . . .

Trollope's novels exemplify that norm of English life; the solid middle class and professional cadre, out of which the substance, if not the rarer flowers, of our national culture has perennially emerged. Its economic range is large. Dickens stands at one end of it, Thackeray and Trollope at another. . . .

There may be in his work a certain reluctance to face the deeper problems of the turmoils and cravings of the human spirit. There are certainly restrictions of sensibility and capacity for nice analysis of motive. These are limitations in the novels of Trollope. But they are limitations general to the majority of people, and their absence is not noticed: just as the presence in Dickens's work of a wild, despairing fantasy is not noticed by the mass of readers. But it is to be observed that Trollope noticed it, and criticized it as something away from the healthy normal after which he strove far more consciously than critics, at least the critics who patronize him, are aware. Hints here and there (as in the character of the Warden himself) reveal in the bluff, masculine character of Trollope something finer, more sharpened, than at first is apparent. It is this that gives his work a distinction, and his characters definition. It makes him a major novelist, one to be signalled among the giants of the nineteenth century, and recognized as no small contributor to the general shape and colour of the English novel. . . .

CHARLOTTE AND EMILY BRONTË

The moment has now come to look at the Brontë family, that parsonage-ful of unaccountable ability, nerves, and ill-health. . . .

Patrick Brontë, a temperamental Irishman, frustrated by some kink in his character from fulfilling his intellectual promise, sunken into morbid self-communion through grief for the loss of his Cornish wife, and left to bring up five daughters and a son in a remote Pennine village, his only neighbours the barbaric mining community, is the central figure on the stage. The four elder girls being sent to a boarding school, two of them died of an epidemic, and the others were brought back to Haworth Rectory, where their education was carried on by themselves, with fitful aid from father, and the errant instruction of wind, rock, and water. The children set up worlds of their own, Charlotte and her brother Branwell (soon to die of drink and boredom) inventing one called *Angria*, a pure fairyland; the other, inhabited by the younger sisters Emily and Anne, a more grim and moral estate called *Gondal*. All of them wrote copiously of adventures in these imaginary countries, the records being kept in microscopic calligraphies, examples of which can now be seen in the British Museum. . . .

The girls turned to professional writing, and in spite of their ignorance of the world, they launched a book of stillborn poems, and then three novels in the year 1847; *Jane Eyre*, by Currer Bell (Charlotte), *Wuthering Heights* by Ellis Bell (Emily), and *Agnes Grey*, by Acton Bell (Anne). Charlotte's book was an instant success, and it led to her being drawn out of the parsonage and introduced to the world, and to her idol Thackeray, to whom she dedicated the second impression of *Jane Eyre*. . . .

Charlotte next tried to take Thackeray's advice to write a novel in the manner of Jane Austen. No doubt he was embarrassed by the completely new element of displayed passion, female passion, in *Jane Eyre;* something hitherto unknown in fiction. . . . While showing the influence of Thackeray, *Villette* is still flooded by the impulsive genius which fills *Jane Eyre;* but in *Villette* this motive force is more controlled, more continuous, more related to the comings and goings of daily human life. For this reason, I find *Villette* the more satisfying novel. *Jane Eyre* is a lyrical poem, the kind of poem written only in adolescence, when excess is all, and restraint is felt to be a self-betrayal.

Still more is this true of *Wuthering Heights*, one of the most odd and unplaceable works in the whole of English fiction. Emily's reliance upon her own inner light was even more marked. The fury of her cravings for she knew not what, forged a handful of primary symbols through which she attempted to interpret the promptings of her nature, at the same time crying out against her failure. The cry is long, wild, eerie, like the mourning of plovers at the end of a savage winter day, a day too short to offer warmth, except for one lurid gleam across the west as the sun goes down unseen. Dying at the age of thirty, Emily was unable to fulfil her promise of powerful intellectual grasp, and an almost Faustian attitude to the world of knowledge and affairs. Certainly this wild tale of spiritual affinity between a girl and a boy, both creatures rebelling against the confines of human nature, would not have been the last attack to come from this remarkable genius. She left also a handful of poems which take their place amongst the most intense utterance in our language. [William] Blake was not more stark. *Wuthering Heights* remains a lonely peak in the landscape of the English novel, where generation after generation of emotional adventurers will climb, to find at the top a handful of scree, a thornbush in the wind, a hawk hovering, and nothing else. The enigma remains, and it is for ever alluring. Matthew Arnold, who had met Charlotte at the house of Quillinan, Wordsworth's son-in-law, two years before her death, wrote an elegy, a lame-rhythm piece, that contains however a fitting description of the enigma in Emily's nature and work.

'How shall I sing her, whose soul
Knew no fellow for might,
Passion, vehemence, grief,
Daring, since Byron died,
That world-famed son of fire—she, who sank
Baffled, unknown, self-consumed;
Whose too bold dying song
Stirr'd, like a clarion-blast, my soul.'

The Victorian Hero

Frederick R. Karl

Frederick R. Karl argues that Victorian novelists created a new kind of male protagonist, not a romantic hero but a decent man without vanity or ego. Victorian characters were, like their predecessors, aware of their station in life, but their virtue is not based on birthright, rather on compassion and civility. Those who failed to live up to these demands were subjected to ridicule and satire—providing Victorian novelists with a source for comedy. Frederick R. Karl, who taught English at the City College of New York, is the author of *A Reader's Guide to Joseph Conrad, The Contemporary English Novel,* and a novel *The Quest.*

Perhaps nowhere more than in the development of the "hero" does the nineteenth-century novelist reveal his basic assumptions. . . .

By the time Jane Austen began to write near the turn of the century, English traditions had weakened and the eighteenth-century gentleman—the redeemed Tom Jones, Squire Allworthy, Matthew Bramble, Walter Shandy, Mr. B., Lovelace[1]—no longer held his undisputed position. The new moneyed classes and increased literacy created a new kind of gentleman: the genteel man of attainments. The stress is now upon what a person is, not solely upon what he has been born into. The gentleman of attainments, further, becomes the sole person capable of holding back the encroaching vulgarity of the industrialized and commercialized middle class, which has no uniform standard of conduct.

QUALITIES REQUIRED OF THE NEW HERO

It is on this frontier of change that Jane Austen places her batteries of wit and irony. Birth, income, and family tradi-

1. characters in eighteenth-century novels

Excerpted from "An Age of Fiction," in *An Age of Fiction: The Nineteenth-Century British Novel,* by Frederick R. Karl. Copyright ©1964 and copyright renewed ©1992 by Frederick R. Karl. Reprinted by permission of Farrar, Straus and Giroux, LLC.

tion, while still important, nevertheless become of secondary significance: the man must still prove himself, for his reputation is not sufficient to make him palatable to a Jane Austen heroine. Like [novelist Fanny Burney's] Evelina with Lord Orville, Elizabeth Bennet is not prepared to accept a proud (somewhat vulgar) Darcy, no less a Mr. B., whom she would mock for his pretensions to supremacy. Jane Austen's heroines themselves desire the kind of equality denied to the eighteenth-century woman, and they demand romantic love as well. Marriage must be prudent, dignified, and romantic. In brief, these clear-eyed girls stand as virtuous individuals with assertive rights. The male can be no undisputed conqueror; he must be civilized and domesticated, brought to heel *before* he offers his name and fortune. The picaresque hero now attends church on Sunday, sips tea in the afternoon, and spends long evenings at home looking through the latest books.

Jane Austen celebrates the rites of happy monogamy, and her standard was to prevail for nearly half a century, with the possible exception of [Emily Brontë's] *Wuthering Heights.* Furthermore, her break with the episodic eighteenth-century novel heralded a similar break throughout the century, although [Charles] Dickens in *Pickwick* followed the form he knew best from his early reading; [William Makepeace] Thackeray also worked in a semi-episodic form in several of his novels, supplying recurring themes, however, to offset episodic stringiness. . . .

The typical Victorian "hero," accordingly, reflects his times. Less grand than his predecessors, he gains virtue from his common sense and compassion. He must be aware of a norm of behavior, as Jane Austen shows us, and if he departs he must be punished before being again accepted. If he departs too far, then he is incorrigible, and he must go into permanent exile or die. If, however, the hero honors social norms—that is, if he lacks ego and vanity—he can gain all, even though his birth and income may be low.

VICTORIAN NOVELISTS ADEPTLY USE THE COMIC SPIRIT

The comic play of the Victorian novel becomes evident as a device for questioning existing standards and for creating social equality. In his essay on Comedy, [George] Meredith remarked that the Comic Spirit would create equality between the sexes; but it does far more. It reveals, and in many cases, purges all anomalies of behavior—whether for good or ill. By exposing the egoistic, the vainglorious, and the snobbish, the Comic Spirit in a burst of ridicule discloses frailties and unmans the offender. As a side effect, unfortunately, it also discourages originality and imagination. In its pursuit of the personally gauche and the socially unacceptable, it tries to reduce all people to the level of social consistency. It leaves little room for the rebel or revolutionary. What Meredith calls the Comic Spirit, Jane Austen incorporated as irony, and the practice extends, in one form or another, through Dickens, Thackeray, and George Eliot, only to fade out and become meaningless in [Thomas] Hardy, who turned the Comic Spirit which mocks foolishness into the Universal Will that condemns all. . . .

Unlike the American novel, the English novel principally takes place in time, not space. Obviously, the temporal novel is most often representative of an old and established culture. It is often a love story, for love is possible when time is plentiful. As soon as time becomes precious, however, love turns to lust. Further, temporal fiction is usually far more realistic than spatial fiction, which is frequently based on the assumption that moving on will bring something better. When the novelist works in a given locale and is aware of the weight of time, he can bring to bear a kind of comic social criticism that all must accept to survive. As soon as characters are given great mobility—as they are in many American novels—there are few common assumptions, and there is accordingly little room for comedy, or for tragedy either. Comedy, like tragedy, then, works on the sharing of suppositions which derive from common traditions. And both depend on time as a factor, for, as the past unfolds, these common assumptions gain the semblance of universal truths. . . .

The stress upon comedy precludes extremism. If, as we have already seen, comedy works to bring deviates back to social norms, then extremism itself can be contained, or else discredited as a viable way of existence. The extremist, when he does exist, usually drifts away or dies of a broken heart; even Emily Brontë—hardly a comic novelist—follows this tradition with Heathcliff. Working in time as he does, the comic novelist allows little flexibility in his major characters. Only in his minor figures, where being "outside" does not seem to matter significantly, can he countenance controlled deviation and extremism. Thus we have the insipidity of so many male protagonists and their sweet ladies in the nineteenth-century novel, while the peripheral, minor figures generate excitement, interest, and humor.

The bourgeois novelist, like many Elizabethan dramatists, developed a double plot with a double standard. While the nineteenth-century audience required certain norms in its "heroes" and "heroines," it tolerantly relaxed these standards (rarely, however, in sexual matters) when the lower classes were concerned. For comic purposes, Dickens often exploited this double standard: gaining raucous fun from the economically deprived, but requiring respectability from his central characters. That he could deploy two such attitudes with both dignity and compassion is a mark of his genius. Similarly, George Eliot gained dramatic tensions from her upper-class characters while she exploited the humor of her peasants.

The comic writer obviously cannot tolerate traditional heroism; the hero depends for sustenance upon his ego, and ego is fair target for the darts of the Comic Spirit. Ego and its twin, Vanity, are the basis for the false gentleman, who loses his status when stringent standards of conduct are applied. Thus, [Dickens's] Joe Gargery is more of a gentleman than Bentley Drummle, and [Eliot's] Adam Bede more than Arthur Donnithorne. Money having become the great equalizer in a commercialized society, standards of excellence came to be based on intrinsic qualities, although a prudent heroine opted for both the true gentleman and a fortune. As Jane Austen demonstrated, prudence and romance are not necessarily alien to each other.

EFFECT OF NEW HERO ON SETTING AND LANGUAGE

With the reduction of the romantic hero to smaller size, there followed a stress upon the details of everyday life. As the genre painters placed man in his setting, so too the nineteenth-century novelist identified his characters through an explicit and detailed background. Jane Austen's provincials—as later George Eliot's—are recognizable people whose lives fit their surroundings: a novel like *Mansfield Park* conveys the flavor of boredom on a respectable country estate, and *Pride and Prejudice* shows that marriage is the sole ritual of maturity when society provides little else for a girl to do. As closely as Jane Austen's characters are identified with their provincial background, so too Dickens's and Thackeray's characters act like city people. The spirit of place is very much a part of Victorian fiction, understandably so once the novel has lost its episodic nature and the action becomes rooted to a particular spot.

Language itself changed to suit the realistic presentation of characters and situations, the movement reaching its culmination in the unselfconscious dialect of George Eliot's and Thomas Hardy's provincials. As the hero becomes a commonplace character, his language loses the rhetorical flourishes and affectations common in the eighteenth century. Declamation turned to slang ([Dickens's] Sam Weller), and speechifying to realistic dialogue ([Eliot's] Adam Bede). Communication was established with a large public unaware of "pretty speech," one attuned to the colloquial language of a relatively urbanized existence.

Characters came to reveal themselves by their talk. Lacking a suitable psychological method and yet aware of the "inner man," the nineteenth-century novelist relied on conversation to disclose the unconscious. This is one reason perhaps why the Victorian novel is full of personalities and the Victorian character seems a person rather than an artificial or fictitious creation. Dickens's characters, for example, are close to the reader because their language reveals submerged details of their personality; they are, as it were, speaking directly to the reader. Although not all nineteenth-century novelists were as aware of their audience as was Dickens, most created intimacy of character and situation through the same personal device of realistic conversation.

The Epic Heritage of *Wuthering Heights*

Vereen Bell

Assistant professor of English at Vanderbilt University Vereen Bell argues that *Wuthering Heights* draws heavily on traditions of storytelling that predate the Victorian formulas of Brontë's day. Brontë's work, he says, embraces folktales and legends of the British Isles and the tradition of oral narrative popular within her own family. Like the best epic poems, Bell explains, Brontë's novel makes powerful use of its storytelling narrator and character monologues. While Brontë's characters remain flat, or undeveloped, Bell says that, as in the world of the ballad, they should not be held up to the "confines of historical definition"; they are successful in that they are psychologically real.

Within its historical context *Wuthering Heights* is remarkable not so much because of its emotional excess as because of the austerity of its design. Without the densely configured social world of earlier English fiction, its realm seems almost oppressively cosmic; its power and intensity are achieved with a sacrifice of human vitality. Yet of course Emily Brontë ignored the conventional human landscape—of inn-keepers and lawyers and thieves—because this was a world which she knew largely nothing about. Her protagonists, whatever they may be symbolically, as social beings are without models and prototypes in our experience. Moreover, because she was intellectually as well as socially isolated, her novel as a whole, like her characters, is distinctly atypical. [Lord David Cecil writes:] "Since she had no ready-made conventions to help her, since she always had to invent them for herself, her form is appropriate to her conception, as it could never have been if she had tried to mold her inspiration to fit the accepted Vic-

Reprinted from Vereen Bell, "The Epic Heritage of *Wuthering Heights*," *College English*, vol. 25, no. 3 (December 1963), pp. 199–208. Reprinted courtesy of the National Council of Teachers of English.

torian formulas." Her most remarkable achievement was in turning her limitations to advantage.

On the other hand *Wuthering Heights* is unique mainly as a hybrid. However little it may have in common with other Victorian fiction, it draws heavily upon older conventions of story, conventions known to Emily Brontë in the fugitive and unprinted folk tales and legends of the British Isles. Within the Brontë family there was a tradition of oral narrative that we are not surprised to find affecting Emily's fiction. Patrick Brontë, we are told, frequently amused his children with lurid tales handed down through his father, Hugh Brunty, an Irish peasant who in his own day had been renowned as a storyteller; and Tabitha Ackroyd, the elderly servant, likewise engaged the children's fancy with tales of fairies and family tragedies. It is not unlikely that a sheltered girl, least tutored of the Brontës, might have found in this familiar genre a natural, easy medium for rendering her conception.

Historically, of course, fiction, as we know it, owes its origins to the [epic] genre—specifically the mode "in which the radical of presentation is the author or minstrel as oral reciter, with a listening audience in front of him"; and in *Wuthering Heights*, a synthesis of spoken narrative conventions with those of the printed page, the novel form is clearly identified with this heritage. In choosing Nelly Dean as her point of view and oral narrative as her medium, Emily Brontë was able to give full expression to her limited creative gift.

NELLY AS STORYTELLER

The dominant structural mode of *Wuthering Heights* is oral—Nelly tells and Lockwood listens—and the narrative's technique is modified and controlled by this peculiar discipline. The nearest familiar analogue is perhaps the English folk ballad. Because of its rigid design the ballad, unlike the novel, must achieve unity of a special kind: "it must forego the novelist's privilege of description and explanation; it must forego . . . the leisure, the comfortable elaboration of the Epic." Nelly's technique is subject to the same conditions; her story is meant to be heard, not read; it must hit hard once and for all. The few symbolic effects of her narrative are sharp and uncomplicated, as they must be, since there is only one chance to convey the desired impression. Over-elaboration lulls the listener and the reader out of awareness.

Without Lockwood there to hear, Nelly would be address-
ing herself directly to the reader, and were that so, she
would be no longer speaking but writing. As a consequence
the whole complexion of her narrative would be altered; she
would incur new responsibilities for detail indigenous to the
novel. As it is, Nelly's sole responsibility is to the central action of her story; anything extraneous is cut away. It is often
remarked, for example, that the reader is always conscious
of the setting of *Wuthering Heights*, and yet the novel is all
but devoid of physical description. The few vivid impres-
sions we do have come from Lockwood. As the recorder he
is aware of his responsibility for placing us securely within
the natural and domestic environment of the action. From
his pen we learn of the exposed, wind-blown station of
Wuthering Heights; of the "stunted firs at the end of the
house," and the "range of gaunt thorns all stretching their
limbs one way, as if craving alms of the sun." Inside the
house his detail is meticulous.

> One end, indeed, reflected splendidly both light and heat
> from ranks of immense pewter dishes, interspersed with sil-
> ver jugs and tankards, towering row after row, in a vast oak
> dresser, to the very roof. The latter had never been under-
> drawn: its entire anatomy lay bare to an inquiring eye, except
> where a frame of wood laden with oatcakes, and clusters of
> legs of beef, mutton, and ham, concealed it. Above the chim-
> ney were sundry villainous old guns, and a couple of horse-
> pistols.

And so on. The style is frankly literary—that is, composed.
In Nelly's simple narrative such elaboration would be implausible and inappropriate; she is confined to strictly relevant external detail. Frequently, for example, she refers to
the elements, but these allusions are always either pertinent
to the action—as when Catherine is stricken from soaking
herself in the rain—or evoked superstitiously in reverie as
rather primitive, symbolic preparation for events of great
moment. . . .

The more extensive and complicated evocations are left to
Lockwood. Because of this division of responsibility, and because Nelly's narrative comprises the major portion of the
book, explicit descriptive setting is naturally and plausibly
scarce. Were Nelly alone in her recollections—composing
instead of speaking—these peripheral descriptions as well
as the central action would fall within her province.

WUTHERING HEIGHTS IS A STORY-CENTERED NOVEL

Moreover, without embroidery, without extra detail, the entire concept of characterization is sharply modified. We can see this discipline at work in the number of characters who figure in Nelly's narrative. Supernumeraries are all but totally absent. Only wholly functional characters appear; all others are severely pared away.

Nelly is responsible directly only to Lockwood, and her range is consequently self-limited. Those figures who we must assume impinged upon the life at Wuthering Heights and the Grange—citizens of nearby Gimmerton, perhaps—she almost wholly ignores. They are not her concern. She has no need for humanizing touches. The linear, relentless progress of events attenuates the shape of her narrative. Unity understood in this narrow sense is rarely encountered in the English novel, and the result in *Wuthering Heights* is a seeming thinness of scope—for all its concentrated impact.

This same discipline has a similar devitalizing effect upon individual character; but the loss in intimacy is more than offset by a corresponding gain in emotional energy and heightened symbolic emphasis. Catherine and Heathcliff are vitalized by the intensity of Emily Brontë's imagination; but as Lord David Cecil has phrased it, they are "more vivid than real." Or in Northrop Frye's language, they are less "real people" than "stylized figures which expand into psychological archetypes"—intensely emotional, perhaps, but stylized just the same. Considering Emily Brontë's limited experience with people and the world, it is not surprising that her central characters are not "real" in any conventional, mimetic sense; but beyond that, the simplicity of the narrative medium, and of its agent Nelly Dean, imposes a kind of aesthetic logic of its own.

Detail is so sparse in Nelly's account that we know next to nothing about the routine of Catherine's and Heathcliff's daily lives. So much is left to the reader's imagination in that quarter that it fails to function at all. Of what Catherine does when she is not tormenting a hapless admirer or lamenting the bitter hostility between Edgar and Heathcliff; of what Heathcliff does with himself when not cursing Catherine or ruining Hindley and the children of three families, we can have no idea. Incident unassociated with the grand torment of Catherine and Heathcliff is discarded as superfluous. It is characteristic of this method that Heathcliff can disappear for years and return to the Heights a wealthy and educated man without the slightest intelligence as to how this transformation was accomplished. Moreover, the limited point of view has again worked to advantage: were we to see Heathcliff, even briefly, in the process of making his fortune, he would necessarily be set into some kind of social and material context; and this definition would almost surely rob him of the essential demonic and archetypal qualities in his character. And of course no one cares where Heathcliff has been or what he has done, just as no reader really cares what happens to the figures when they are off-stage; the story itself is too absorbing, the emotional pitch too high for distractions to be desirable. But this very tautness points up the fact that *Wuthering Heights* is, after all, like the ballad, not character-centered but story-centered; the action determines how much we are to see of a given individual.

BRONTË'S CHARACTERS ARE PSYCHOLOGICALLY REAL

In a sense Emily Brontë's figures are flat characters, to use Forster's term, but this is not to say that they do not develop. With Catherine, for example, all but the most essential elements of character are refined away. Yet she is by no means static: time wears patiently at her wayward disposition, and when she dies, a haggard, beaten, and bewildered woman, she is far removed from the impetuous but compassionate spirit we knew as a girl. Heathcliff and Catherine, young Cathy and Hareton are all highly refined conceptions, and when time passes over them it is not to open new possibilities of personality, but to shape and maim those few given us at the start—only those in fact that are essential to the story. Because the story is made to be heard it must be delivered in the simplest and most vivid accents.

The struggle of Heathcliff and Catherine to merge their identities Nelly develops (in the ballad tradition) through a series of linked scenes. She is not above summarizing a period of three years or twelve, but these summary passages are brief, often barely a sentence, and the scenes are long. They are also revealing. There can be, of course, none of Dickens' elaboration of recurrent gesture, the leitmotifs that assist us in immediate recognition; nor is Nelly attentive to the efficacy or personal idiom, except with Joseph, whom even Isabella mocks as a sort of standing joke and who is very little else than an idiomatic Yorkshire chorus. As a consequence, though we may see the characters directly for the most part, we have some difficulty in conceiving for them a distinct social image.

Psychologically, however, they are fully known. Nelly has not the intellectual equipment for analysis, but her faithful (if improbable) rendering of dialogue does the job for her. She has no access to self-communings, but the scenes are selected with such care that private doubts and frustrations are repeatedly and emphatically suggested in dramatic action. So while we perceive only the essential aspect of character, that vital spirit is revolved about and centered upon until the inner conflict is forcefully dramatized. Typical of these revealing incidents is the significant scene that discloses young Heathcliff's apprehension when it appears that the bond between him and Catherine is about to be severed. Catherine is expecting her young friends from across the moor; when Heathcliff inquires pointedly about her silk frock she is at first evasive but finally finds it needful "to smooth the way for an intrusion."

> "Isabella and Edgar Linton talked of calling this afternoon. . . . As it rains, I hardly expect them; but, they may come, and if they do, you run the risk of being scolded for no good."
> "Order Ellen to say you are engaged, Cathy," he persisted. "Don't turn me out for those pitiful, silly friends of yours! I'm on the point, sometimes, of complaining that they—but I'll not—"
> "That they what?" cried Catherine, gazing at him with a troubled countenance. "Oh, Nelly!" she added petulantly, jerking her head away from my hands, "You've combed my hair quite out of curl! That's enough, let me alone. What are you on the point of complaining about, Heathcliff?"
> "Nothing—only look at the almanack, on that wall." He pointed to a framed sheet hanging near the window, and continued:
> "The crosses are for the evenings you have spent with the Lintons, the dots for those spent with me. Do you see? I've marked every day."
> "Yes—very foolish; as if I took notice!" replied Catherine in a peevish tone. "And where is the sense of that?"
> "To show you that I *do* take notice," said Heathcliff.
> "And should I always be sitting with you?" she demanded. . . . "What good do I get—what do you talk about? You might be dumb or a baby for anything you say to amuse me, or for anything you do, either!"
> "You never told me before that I talked too little, or that you

disliked my company, Cathy!" exclaimed Heathcliff in much agitation.

"It's no company at all, when people know nothing and say nothing," she muttered.

Here the scene is broken off by the entrance of Edgar Linton. Nothing is resolved; the painful tension is left unrelieved. But when this scene is merged easily with another in the next instant, the full effect upon Catherine becomes apparent. Unable to suppress her guilt, she explodes violently when Nelly seems impertinent, turns savagely upon little Hareton, and even strikes Linton when he tries to interfere. When she finally relieves her stress in tears, the reader is released momentarily to reflect and know the full meaning of Catherine's conflict between boundless love and the obstruction to its fulfillment in her and Heathcliff's disparate temperaments.

The Power of Monologue

Dialogue, however, only suggests what is beneath the surface; to penetrate deeper, to explore the more subtle psychological and emotional states that are only intimated in dramatic action, Emily Brontë resorts to an adroit use of monologue, and, again to Nelly's faithful reporting. We are permitted to view another dimension of Catherine's character in several scenes in which Catherine almost unconsciously purges herself in a kind of compulsive articulation. Of such are Catherine's words in the aftermath of the reunion with Heathcliff and the terrible foredooming encounter with her unsympathetic husband. Distractedly she examines the feathers of her pillow torn with her teeth in a fit of frenzy.

> "That's a turkey's," she murmured to herself; "and this is a wild duck's; and this is a pigeon's. Ah, they put pigeons' feathers in the pillows—no wonder I couldn't die! Let me take care to throw it on the floor when I lie down. And here's a moorcock's; and this—I should know it among a thousand—it's a lapwing's. Bonny bird; wheeling over our heads in the middle of the moor. It wanted to get to its nest, for the clouds touched the swells, and it felt rain coming. This feather was picked up from the heath, the bird was not shot—we saw its nest in the winter, full of little skeletons. Heathcliff set a trap over it, and the old ones dare not come. I made him promise he'd never shoot a lapwing, after that, and he didn't. Yes, there are more! Did he shoot my lapwings, Nelly? Are they red, any of them?"

Symbolically in these words Catherine describes the tragedy of her existence—the tension between her will to freedom and her need of security, and finally Heathcliff's determined refusal to permit her to come to rest. Many years later the bird image recurs to disclose, ironically, precisely the opposite yearning of young Cathy's flickering spirit. A sullen, beaten prisoner in the dark household of Heathcliff, she sits alone, carving out of turnip parings "figures of birds and beasts." When Lockwood enlivens her somewhat with news of Nelly and home, she gazes distantly at the hills and murmurs with simple eloquence, "I should like to be riding Minny down there! I should like to be climbing up there— Oh! I'm tired—I'm *stalled*, Hareton!"

ECHOING THE EPIC

As a narrator Nelly makes the best of her limited opportunities. She does not embroider; her development is linear and pure; but it is always emphatically and sharply centered. The subtle currents of emotional energy are so tautly sustained that our disbelief is suspended, and Heathcliff's and Catherine's anguished love, intense beyond the sphere of social reality, is made both convincing and moving. Ultimately the inadvertent discipline of [the epic] works to advantage. Nelly cannot give us enough detail, Dickens-data, of telling gesture and idiom to individualize her people very sharply. They have not the hard edges of a social image. What is accomplished, however, is a fine balance between social and symbolic character. The inherent restrictions of her medium give us characters who are not so distinct, not so particularized as individuals that they cannot be easily extended outward into mythic figures; and yet they are not so highly abstracted that we cannot feel their pain and understand in them new depths of human suffering. The two concepts of characterization enforce each other; the human quality enforces the symbolic by adding the cogency of identification; the symbolic enforces the human by extending one strange event of history into the more enduring realm of myth. Both results are accomplished through an artful modification of traditional techniques of oral narrative. . . .

Like the ballad, Nelly's tale is not concerned with society at large but with an imprecise, fugitive world of its own and this concentration has the effect of releasing her characters from the confines of historical definition.

Again like the ballad, as the figures are independent of time they are also immune to ethical judgment. Nelly, it is true, utters opinions, but she is a character of the action, independent of the author's views and obviously not to be taken as a persona; her morality is patently superficial and therefore inadequate. Nelly's judgment is there in fact only to show how facile and incompetent human judgment can be. The love of Heathcliff and Catherine transcends all human standards of behavior; and by presenting their tragedy through one who has her own view Emily Brontë avoids taking on the responsibility for attempting the impossible, that is, passing an ultimate God-like judgment herself. Unappraised by a superior human intellect, Heathcliff and Catherine are left to move outside the moral realm. Nelly cannot pull them down to her level; her imagination does not soar. But she gives them life, and once they breathe they generate their own strength to transcend not only human values but the confines of life itself.

Female Independence in *Jane Eyre*

Erica Jong

In the introduction to the Penguin edition of *Jane Eyre*, Erica Jong writes that Charlotte Brontë was ahead of her time in her creation of the unforgettable heroine Jane. Brontë, according to Jong, convincingly—if not consciously—portrays a woman who refuses to succumb to the rules and strictures imposed on nineteenth-century women. Rather, Jane's strivings are remarkably modern: With unswerving courage, Jane breaks the conventions of Victorian society in her quest for independence, self-respect, and a love relationship based on equality. Jong, the author of six best-selling novels, speaks frequently on issues that affect women.

When a book is beloved by readers and hated by contemporary critics, we should suspect that a revolution in consciousness is in progress. This was certainly the case with *Jane Eyre*. The pseudonymous author, Currer Bell, was blamed for committing the "highest moral offence a novel writer can commit, that of making an unworthy character interesting in the eyes of a reader." The book was said to be mischievous and vulgar, pandering to the public's taste for "illegitimate romance." As for the character of the heroine, "Jane Eyre is throughout the personification of an unregenerate and undisciplined spirit . . . she has inherited in fullest measure the worst sin of our fallen nature—the sin of pride."

These criticisms were put forth by a woman reviewer, Elizabeth Rigby, in *The Quarterly Review* in 1848, four years after the novel was published, when it was already a roaring success. The same critic took pains to dispute the rumor that Currer Bell was a woman, explaining that the descriptions of cookery and fashion could not have come from a female pen.

She also argued that the book would do more harm than good to governesses, and for good measure, she condemned Jane Eyre as one "whom we should not care for as an acquaintance, whom we should not seek as a friend, whom we should not desire for a relation, and whom we should scrupulously avoid for a governess."

Such character assassinations would be too absurd to quote if they did not foreshadow the charges against every important novel of the nineteenth and twentieth centuries that depicted a woman as a complex human being rather than a stereotype. More than that, they foreshadow contemporary assaults on women's anger, rebellion, and nonconformity—whether exemplified in fiction or in life. For Jane is nothing if not a rebel. She will not lie even if lies would smooth her progress. From the moment we meet her, she is struggling against the injustice of her lot, and she refuses to be convinced that humility is her only option. In many ways she is the first modern heroine in fiction.

Self-Respect

The perennial popularity of *Jane Eyre* with readers is surely based on Jane's indomitable spirit. Given every reason to feel crushed, discouraged, beaten, Jane's will remains unbroken. Neither beautiful nor rich nor supplied with a cossetting family, Jane seems to be possessed of the greatest treasure a woman can have: self-respect. That alone makes her an inspiring heroine. No one can take away her inner self-esteem. It is apparent from the very start of the book, when ten-year-old Jane tells her supposed "benefactress" Mrs. Reed (who has unjustly punished her by secluding her from her cousins): "They are not fit to associate with me." We love Jane because she seems to know her own worth— an unforgivable thing in girls and women.

It is her grittiness that saves her at Lowood school, where punishments are meted out unfairly and girls are sent to starve and sicken. Helen, who meekly accepts unjust punishments, dies. Jane survives because she does not. In fact, it is remarkable how often Jane says the thing she knows she should not as if overcome by an irresistible force. She is active where all her training tells her to be passive. She speaks the truth when she is supposed to flatter. She longs for the wide world when she is supposed to be content with her narrow lot. "I could not help it; the restlessness was in my nature," she says, pacing "backwards and forwards" on the third story of Thornfield Hall. "Women feel just as men feel," Jane says, "they need exercise for their faculties and a field for their efforts."

When a book has been copied as much as *Jane Eyre*, has spawned as many bad imitations, movies, adaptations, it's necessary to go back to the text and try to see it as if for the first time. What has usually been imitated about this novel is not the spirit of the heroine but the gloomy house with its dark secret, its glowering hero, and the star-crossed romance of its two principal characters. These strike me as the *least* important elements of the story. If Jane were a passive heroine, neither the romantic battlements of gloomy Thornfield nor the curmudgeonly charms of Mr. Rochester would capture us. But Jane's bluntness, the modernity of her strivings for independence, invite us into the tale. From the first instant we meet Jane Eyre, we know she is a different breed.

As a novelist, what interests me most about *Jane Eyre* is the way Charlotte Brontë transformed autobiographical materials to create a myth that is larger and more powerful than any of its parts. Apparently Charlotte and her siblings did have a forbidding aunt who attempted without success to replace their dead mother. Apparently they were sent away to a harsh charity school not unlike Lowood. Apparently, Charlotte did fall in love with a married man—M. Heger, the headmaster of the school in Brussels where Charlotte, for a time, taught. But the way Charlotte *changed* these materials is far more interesting than the way the facts agree with her autobiography. She sets the struggle not in a school in Brussels but in a foreboding North of England country house where the restless master comes and goes. The house represents the fate of woman in the nineteenth century: enclosure, entrapment, no hope of escape. Not only Jane is captive there, but so is Jane's alter ego, Bertha Mason, the mad wife in the attic. And the mystery revolves around the discovery of the mad wife, whose existence is denied even when her rages threaten the lives of those in the house.

ENTRAPPED WOMANHOOD

It was Charlotte Brontë's genius to find a threefold representation of nineteenth-century woman: the feisty Jane, the animalistic Bertha, the mansion that is destined to burn down because of its incendiary contents. If Bertha is sexuality denied, then Jane is freedom denied, but they are both aspects of entrapped womanhood. Thornfield Hall itself represents the outdated rules imposed on women—which cannot endure any more than a house with a trapped madwoman can.

Surely all these symbols were unconscious with the author. Otherwise she could not have made them so convincing. But the unconscious of an artist is her greatest treasure. It is what transmutes the dross of autobiography into the gold of myth.

Jane Eyre takes the form of a pilgrimage in which a little girl who is old before her time from being reared in the most constricted of circumstances gradually finds a way to blossom. But first she must submit to many tests. She must reject a variety of hypocritical masculine figures who feel it is their right to rule her. She must reject the fate of being a female victim—the only model presented to her by other women. She must reject the entreaties of her potential lover until he has been transformed by his own purifying odyssey.

To be the equal of Jane Eyre, Rochester must renounce all other women, see his patrimony go up in flames, lose an eye and a hand, and become grateful where he once was arrogant. Only when he has been thus transformed can he and Jane have a happily-ever-after.

Charlotte Brontë's brilliance was to create a myth which is the embodiment of female wish fulfillment. The universe of *Jane Eyre* operates according to female laws. Jane's success as a heroine depends on her breaking all the rules decreed for nineteenth-century women. Outspoken where she should be submissive, bold where she should be grateful— apparently nobody has told Jane Eyre that she is plainer than Cinderella's step-sisters and has no business turning down a rich suitor before she knows she is an heiress herself. This is a fairy tale that reverses all the rules of fairy tales. No wonder it strikes readers as a burst of light into the heart of darkness.

DREAMS AND VISIONS

To a remarkable extent, the novel relies on the heroine's sensitivity to dreams and visions—as if the author were saying that only a woman in touch with her deepest dreams can be a strong survivor in a world so toxic to women. Dreams are crucial in *Jane Eyre*. The night before Jane is to marry the already married Rochester, she prophetically dreams that "Thornfield Hall was a dreary ruin, the retreat of bats and owls." The house is reduced to "a shell-like wall, very high and fragile-looking," and Jane wanders there with an unknown child in her arms.

Perhaps the child in the dream represents the innocence that she is soon to lose: At church the next day, the wedding is canceled when Rochester's bigamy is revealed. Because he thinks of Bertha Mason as a "clothed hyena" whom he was entrapped into marrying, Rochester has no qualms about betraying his mad wife. But Jane, though she loves him, refuses to be drawn into his error. He married Bertha for her money, and that falsehood is not so easily cured. In this female universe, a man is not forgiven for a cynical marriage even if it is the rule in his society. So Jane, though heartbroken, leaves Thornfield Hall. She wanders in the dark woods of her destiny, finds she is an heiress herself, is commandeered in marriage by another man (the dour parson, St. John) while Rochester's soul is being shriven.

Rochester may be arrogant and full of male entitlement, but he is not cold and calculating like St. John. In fact, it is St. John who evokes in Jane the certainty that she can only marry for love. He wants Jane because she will make a good missionary in India, not because he loves her. This Jane feels as "an iron shroud contracted round me." She can't allow herself to be with a man whose brow is "commanding but not open," whose eyes are "never soft." By refusing to marry him, "I should still have my unblighted self to turn to: my natural unenslaved feelings with which to communicate in moments of loneliness. There would be recesses in my mind which would be only mine." As his wife she would become "the imprisoned flame" consumed from within.

Jane may be the first heroine in fiction to know that she needs her own identity more than she needs marriage. Her determination not to relinquish selfhood for love could well belong to a contemporary heroine.

Jane can only return to Rochester when she can say: "I am an independent woman now." And she can only surrender to him when he says: "All the melody on earth is concentrated in Jane's tongue to my ear." "The water stood in my eyes to hear the avowal of his dependence," Jane says. And indeed she cannot marry Rochester until he knows he is as dependent on her as she is on him. Their odysseys have equalized them: Jane has become an independent woman and Rochester has been cured of entitlement. Only thus can a woman and man become equals in a patriarchal society.

We are drawn to those myths that speak the truth we know about our inner lives. *Jane Eyre* endures because it tells the truth about what makes a marriage of two minds possible. The shoe fits—far better than Cinderella's glass slipper. Men must be stripped of arrogance and women must become independent for any happily-ever-after to endure between the sexes. Charlotte Brontë's unconscious was way ahead of her time.

Dickens: The Epitome of the Victorian Age

S. Diana Neill

S. Diana Neill weaves together information about Dickens's life with commentary about sixteen of his works to show that Dickens epitomizes his era. She describes the horror of his childhood experience working in the blacking factory and explains its effects on his outlook and works. Neill concludes by summarizing four phases of Dickens's writing, identifying major elements that characterize each. S. Diana Neill was extension lecturer in adult education at the University of London. She is the author of critical essays analyzing Victorian novelists.

The literary giant best fitted to feed this voracious, if inhibited, public was Charles Dickens, a sturdy individualist of no great depth of thought, but richly endowed with creative energy and showmanship. Dickens stands, by reason of the superb range of his characters, unrivalled among English novelists and invites comparison with [French novelist Honoré de] Balzac and [Russian novelist Fyodor] Dostoievski. Dickens is immortal because he is so essentially of his time. . . .

Dickens did not possess the power of divining the inner workings of his age but he succeeded in reflecting from a thousand facets its temporary saliences.[1] It was an exciting, melodramatic, warmhearted, prodigal age, and Dickens was part of it. No other novelist showed such a gift for getting inside the skins of so many characters. Everything he touched came to life beneath his hand or seemed to, although today it may appear to some that what he endowed with the magic of life was in reality a puppet show—macabre and tinselled. As the Victorian age recedes into the past it can only be evoked

1. most conspicuous, most prominent parts

Excerpted from S. Diana Neill, *A Short History of the English Novel* (London: Jarrolds, 1951).

through literature, and the image that sprawls in the pages of Dickens is fantastic and distorted. Perhaps the origin of this distortion must be sought in certain experiences of his life. . . .

A Childhood Experience Affects Dickens's Life and His Novels

In February 1824 his father was arrested for debt and carried off to the Marshalsea Prison. The situation of the family was serious; there was no money to buy bread and the boy was forced to pawn his precious books one by one. But worse was to come—an experience so bitter and humiliating that it continued to haunt him long after his genius had won for him a place in society denied him by his birth. His parents found a job for him in Warren's blacking factory, owned by a relative. For six months, in utter despair at the eclipse of his dreams, Dickens, still little more than a child, worked in the dirty, rat-infested old house down by the river—sticking labels on blacking bottles. To get the utmost benefit from the light that filtered through the dusty air the boys stood near the windows, where they aroused the interest of passers-by. This was the first raw impact of life on the sensitive nerves of a boy who had lived in the dream world of elegance and polite learning. . . .

His own adolescent sufferings were turned to good account many years later in the semi-autobiographical *David Copperfield;* but a great and universal pity for the poor and downtrodden had been awakened in him which was to provide the driving power behind his pen in book after book. It is also probable that the violence and sadism in his novels had their origin in the unresolved psychological tensions of this period, in the shock of disillusionment and in the emotional conflicts occasioned by his attitude to his parents.

His sufferings did not make him a rebel against society. He was perhaps born too soon for that. Nor is there a *fin-de-siècle*[2] longing for escape. No ivory tower claimed him, and Dickens did not turn away from a system that seemed to crush all human aspiration towards goodness and beauty. Instead he set out to reform the system through pity and laughter, but the topical purpose effectively limited his powers as an artist. . . .

---

2. characteristic of the last part of the nineteenth century

PICKWICK LAUNCHES DICKENS'S CAREER AND HIS POPULARITY

In 1836 he was asked by Chapman and Hall, the publishers, to write the letterpress for a set of cockney sporting prints which a popular artist, Seymour, was to illustrate. Having to rely almost entirely on imagination, for Dickens had no sporting memories or experiences, he hit upon the idea of inventing a genial, innocent and lovable old gentleman, Mr. Pickwick, who was to become world-famous as the founder of a club of harmless lunatics. . . .

After four or five parts of Mr. Pickwick's adventures had appeared the work suddenly sprang into popularity which each succeeding part carried higher and higher. Four hundred copies of the first part were prepared, but for the fifteenth forty thousand copies were needed. The British public took the club of harmless lunatics to its bosom, repeated what the members said, quoted them, appealed to their judgments, and found itself confirmed and strengthened. The Pickwickians had become a national institution, and 'Dickensian' humour passed into the language. Dickens's pen was, like [Walter] Scott's, a fertile one. No sooner had a vein of fiction been opened up than it seemed inexhaustible. The immense vitality he poured into his books made them seem—as [critic and novelist] G.K. Chesterton has said—less like separate novels than lengths cut from the flowing and mixed substances called Dickens. In such a generous harvest there are inevitably tares among the wheat—stagey characters, slapdash work, and, to a later generation, serious lapses of taste.

Pickwick had been an essay in pure humour, a series of entertaining episodes lightly strung together. But Dickens was aware of the contrast between the atavistic[3] memories they evoked and the cruelty and injustice in the world around him. In the novels that followed *Pickwick* he took on the familiar role of the crusader. His aim was to wring the conscience of society by playing upon its feelings and presenting scenes of harrowing misery that could be shown as the outcome of personal indifference and social callousness.

It must be remembered that what seems today the overdrawn and laboured sentimentality of his children's deathbed scenes wrung the hearts of his own contemporaries.

3. nostalgic

Looking back and speaking through the mouth of David Copperfield, with complete simplicity, Dickens explained his own success and his own philosophy: "Whatever I have tried to do in life, I have tried with all my heart to do well." If heart, rather than judgment, is taken as a criterion, even the death-beds are understandable.

DICKENS'S FIRST-PHASE NOVELS

As a crusader for the oppressed, Dickens first attacked the stony-heartedness of organized charity. In *Oliver Twist* (1838) he showed that the Poor Law Reform Act had only strengthened institutionalism by giving authority to unkindness. In Mr. Bumble all selfish dispensers of public charity stand condemned, and in *Oliver Twist* their helpless victims find an eternal symbol. For Oliver to have become a national byword as the small boy who dared to ask for a second helping is a measure of the impact of his story on the well-fed and complacent reading public. An even worse shock was to come later, in *Bleak House*, when young Jo, typifying the utterly destitute everywhere, dies of hunger. "Dead," said Dickens, the moralizer, of his little crossing-sweeper. "Dead, Right Reverends and Wrong Reverends of every order. Dead, men and women born with Heavenly compassion in your hearts. And dying thus around us every day."

Nicholas Nickleby (1839) exposed the goings-on behind the doors of private schools. Next came *The Old Curiosity Shop* (1840), perhaps best remembered for the overstrained emotionalism of the death of Little Nell—the angel child, too good to live, a scene which provided contemporary readers with one of the highlights of fiction, but which a less sentimental age has damned to perdition. To offset the pathos of the child and her loving but wretched grandfather we have the creation of Quilp, a character impregnated with malice and wearing physical ugliness as the outward sign of spiritual repulsiveness.

A visit to America in 1842 resulted in bitter disappointment for Dickens. He had expected too much. There in a free republican State he believed he would meet with more natural goodness, equality and justice than he saw at home. Instead he found disgusting manners, a crudity that repelled him and a venality unrivalled even in Europe. *Martin Chuzzlewit* (1844) records his disillusionment. American scenes in it gave offence, but the book is memorable for its characters.

Sarah Gamp ("He'd make a lovely corpse"), Tom Finch, the Franciscan Mark Tapley, and that prince of hypocrites Pecksniff, make the novel a favourite with English readers. . . .

By 1850 Dickens had added to his output the Christmas Tales including *A Christmas Carol* (1843), *Dombey and Son* (1848) and *David Copperfield* (1849–50). The first of these is Dickens's touchstone. It is a miracle play. The little cripple, Tiny Tim, is not a real little boy like David, puzzled, loving and trying to learn his way about the world. He is youth and innocence personified, just as Scrooge typifies the lovelessness of the miser. In the warm glow of the Christmas spirit, ugliness and evil vanish, and Scrooge is transformed by the all-pervading benevolence and goodwill in the very air about him. . . .

The earlier novels had been constructed to no very definite plan. They are mostly picaresque, the hero acting as the connecting link between one episode and the next. In *Dombey and Son* there is a central theme. It is not so much the sombre figure of Mr. Dombey who holds the story together, as the cold pride of Mr. Dombey—destroying the lives of those with whom he comes in contact. There is considerable poetic imagination and truth in the scene in the desolate house, where Dombey is left alone, the muddy footmarks which symbolize his own path through life, as he has trampled on the affection of his daughter, Flo, in revenge for the loss of his son, Paul.

Of *David Copperfield* Dickens wrote: "I like this one the best," and the novel may be regarded as a veiled autobiography. In the chapters covering David Copperfield's childhood Dickens showed an imaginative understanding of the child's point of view that was new in literature. The bewilderment of a little boy, at the mercy of adult decisions and their unpredictable whims, is described with a tenderness which must have surprised families where well-brought-up children were locked in dark cupboards for the slightest display of 'naughtiness'.

DICKENS'S SECOND-PHASE NOVELS

Bleak House, which followed in 1853, is a tragedy which, in tragic intensity, far surpasses the gloomy history of Mr. Dombey. Suggested by the celebrated proceedings arising from the estate of one William Jennings, who died in 1798, leaving property at Birmingham worth many millions, the case of Jarndyce and Jarndyce is a commentary, at once tragic and satiric, on the abuses of the old courts of Chancery, the delays and costs of which brought misery and ruin on its suitors. The plot is intricately woven, and the central theme so skilfully used, that every episode and every character has something to contribute to the inexorable chain of events leading towards the exposure of Lady Dedlock. But surpassing this is the force of symbolism in the novel. In fact in this sombre story of hearts worn to despair and minds driven to madness by the inscrutable injustice and infinite delays of the Law there is much to recall the world of Dostoievsky, while the powerful intensity with which symbol and plot are fused is reminiscent of [Austrian novelist Franz] Kafka.

From the physical fog that blots out the city Dickens passes to the dreadful nights of spiritual darkness that is at its thickest and most terrible in the workings of a system of Law that has lost touch with human needs.

"Fog everywhere. Fog up the river, where it flows among green aits⁴ and meadows; fog down the river, where it rolls defiled among the tiers of shipping, and the waterside pollutions of a great (and dirty) city. Fog on the Essex marshes, fog on the Kentish heights. Fog creeping into the cabooses of the collier-brigs; fog lying out in the yards, and hovering in the rigging of great ships; fog dropping on the gunwales of barges and small boats. . . .

"Gas looming through the fog in divers places in the streets, much as the sun may, from the spongy fields, be seen to loom by husbandmen and ploughboy. Most of the shops lighted two hours before their time—as the gas seems to know, for it has a haggard and unwilling look.

"The raw afternoon is rawest, and the dense fog is densest and the muddy streets are muddiest, near that leaden-headed old corporation: Temple Bar. And hard by Temple Bar, in Lincoln's Inn Hall, at the very heart of the fog, sits the Lord High Chancellor in his High Court of Chancery. Never can there come fog too thick, never can there come mud and mire too deep, to assort with the groping and floundering condition which this High Court of Chancery, most pestilent of hoary sinners, holds, this day, in the sight of heaven and earth."

Through the fog of frustration and throughout the book the two Wards in Chancery, and others connected with them, grope their way. Poor little Miss Flite has already lost

4. small islands

her reason, and gradually it becomes clear that as Richard Carstone's golden optimism wavers towards despair, he too will be driven mad, or rather that he will escape into madness from an unbearable agony of uncertainty. For

> "This is the Court of Chancery; which has its decaying houses and its blighted land in every shire; which has its worn-out lunatic in every madhouse, and its dead in every churchyard; which has its ruined suitor, with his slipshod heels and threadbare dress, borrowing and begging through the round of every man's acquaintance; which gives to monied might, the means of wearying out the right; which so exhausts finances, patience, courage, hope; so overthrows the brain and breaks the heart; that there is not an honourable man among its practitioners who would not give—who does not often give—the warning, 'Suffer any wrong that can be done you rather than come here!'"

Dickens the social reformer tilted at the vast, apathetic and incomprehensible web woven by a legal system that had lost touch with reality; but the story seems to have taken possession of him and far surpasses the original purpose. It also inspired him to the creation of some of his best characters. Dickens, often so unsuccessful with the delineation of educated men and women, has several in this book who are more or less convincing. The best of all is Sir Leicester Dedlock—ludicrous, stiff and inarticulate, but in his utter moral integrity by no means a caricature of the English ruling classes. The suave lawyer Tulkinghorn and the shy philanthropist Mr. Jarndyce are both rather more than types. There are a host of interesting minor characters, among whom may be mentioned Harold Skimpole, drawn from [essayist] Leigh Hunt, who disguises his complete selfishness under a guise of childish irresponsibility. The irascible yet generous Boythorn, with his canary, is drawn from [essayist and poet] Walter Savage Landor.

Dickens's powers of characterization were limited. Apart from the obviously stagey and melodramatic figures, he is apt to carry the reader away by sheer quantitative achievement. On closer analysis many of his immortal creations turn out to be not real persons, but brilliantly sketched personifications of vices and virtues, reminiscent of the 'humours' of [Renaissance poet and playwright] Ben Jonson. In *Bleak House*, however, even a minor character like Mrs. Bagnet is not just a soldier's wife; she is Mrs. Bagnet and nobody else. Sometimes it is hard to differentiate. Mrs. Jellyby might

be a type—the kind of woman who neglects her home in order to work for a mission to Borrioboola-Gha; but again
Dickens's intense powers of observation and love of detail
come in to save her. She is unique as the slatternly house-
wife whose curtains were skewered back with forks!

In *Hard Times* (1854), a novel instinct with power, he returned to the attack on the industrial evils of his day, epito-
mizing in Coketown all industrial towns and in the Grad-
grinds and the Bounderbys showing up the inhuman
representatives of the system of enlightened self-interest that
had only theory to recommend it.

The target in *Little Dorrit* (1857) is the unreformed Civil
Service, with its nepotism and its injustices. Here the dice are
loaded against the Circumlocution Offices and the human
Barnacles who make the system work but whose selfishness
and indifference destroy the soul in the society they serve.

With *A Tale of Two Cities* (1859) Dickens returned to the
historical novel, a genre which he had already essayed in
Barnaby Rudge, a story of the Gordon Riots.[5] His limitations
are soon disclosed when he strays outside the magic London
circle in which he conjured up his fantastic rout. His attitude
to the French Revolution suggests the fundamental dualism
at the root of Dickens's political convictions, which made
him, for instance, although a radical, an opponent of the
Chartists[6] because he hated physical violence. "The aristo-
crats deserved all they got, but the passion engendered in
the people by the misery and starvation replaced one set of
oppressors by another." His sympathies were with the suffering, but he feared violence, for it stirred in him deep-
rooted emotional complexes that had their origin in his adolescence and had never been resolved.

To the last phase of Dickens's literary career belongs
Great Expectations (1861), a work regarded by many critics
as his best. The story of the benevolent convict, young Pip,
the proud Estella and the tragically eccentric Miss Hav-
isham is well told, while the description of the Great Salt
Marsh where Pip first meets the convict creates an atmosphere of cold horror that challenges comparison with
[Thomas] Hardy's study of Egdon Heath in *The Return of the
Native.*

---

5. led by anti-Catholic Lord George Gordon in 1780; mobs pillaged and burned pro-
testing the conditions of the working poor   6. Chartists, the first working-class movement, demanded suffrage and other voter rights.

Three years later came *Our Mutual Friend* (1864), a mellow and charming book, noteworthy for the interesting character of the schoolmaster, Bradley Headstone, the first murderer in Dickens to exhibit any complexity of character. And he is the first to present himself as a member of respectable Victorian society. The novel contains a dreadful and convincing picture of the double life led by Bradley Headstone as he goes about his duties as a schoolmaster after he has decided to murder Eugene, for whom the woman he loves has manifested a preference.

DICKENS'S LAST UNFINISHED NOVEL

At the time of his premature death in 1870 Dickens was working on what might be called a psychological thriller, *The Mystery of Edwin Drood*. Eastern influences which were beginning to affect literature are seen in the character of Jasper Drood, the opium-smoker, Kali-worshipper, and choirmaster and precentor of Cloisterham Cathedral. This is one of Dickens's more complex character-studies, and may contain much unconscious self-analysis. Perhaps Dickens comes near to revealing the split in his own personality in emphasizing Jasper's two states of consciousness that never clash, but each of which pursues its separate course as though it were continuous instead of broken.

The murderer, Drood, has lived all his life in an atmosphere of sanctity, worshipping the Christian God, singing hymns and directing the devotions of others, but his other self has surrendered to the enchantment of evil, embodied in an alien civilization, drugs, and hallucinations. Oddly enough, Dickens had spent his life writing novels full of goodwill, sentiment, high spirits and kindliness, but the most vivid experiences related in them were all inspired by evil, violence, malignity, cruelty. It has been suggested that Dickens himself was perhaps caught between two classes of society as the choirmaster between two civilizations, and in both cases the conflict resulted in a strong impulse to destroy. Dickens the artist sublimated his evil passions in the nerve-torturing scenes of sadism he depicted; Drood committed murder.

All his life Dickens drove himself hard—perhaps too hard. At the height of his fame he was not only writing and editing, but also giving dramatic readings from his books in both England and America. These brought him money and also a certain emotional satisfaction. In the idolatrous applause of a vast audience, throbbing with excitement as he threw all his considerable histrionic skill into making them see the death of Bill Sykes or the murder of Nancy, Dickens found the anodyne he needed to soothe past hurts that time had hidden but not healed.

His death was sudden and dramatic. On 9 June, 1870, he had put in a long day on *Edwin Drood,* when he had a stroke while he was eating dinner. He got up from the table in his stunned condition and said he must go to London; then he fell to the floor and never recovered consciousness. He died the next afternoon.

DICKENS HIGHLIGHTS: HUMOUR, CHARACTERS, ENTERTAINMENT, AND OPTIMISM

Perhaps Dickens's major contribution to literature, that which gives him his rank among the giants, was his discovery of new sources of humour. Like [eighteenth-century novelist Tobias George] Smollett, the greatest literary influence on him, he saw the humour of funny faces. A child who was asleep in a room in which Dickens was writing later recalled how, waking up suddenly, she saw the novelist make faces at himself in the looking-glass and then return to his desk and continue his work.

He was delighted, too, by the humour of odd tricks of speech, like the jerky, machine-gunning staccato conversation of Mr. Jingle, and the ungrammatical circumlocutions of the uneducated in sentences from which they can only extricate themselves by means of more and more relative clauses. He went far beyond Smollett in the supreme sophistication which can see childish fun in the contrariness of inanimate objects. The 'veskitt' button that won't button was something new in English literature—it suggests something of the Russian [novelist Nikolai Vasilevich] Gogol. Dickens exploited to the full the absurdity of the apt or ludicrously unsuitable name, and he loved to mock the humour of the professional outlook—the overriding egotism which makes an undertaker say that a beautiful funeral is something to "reconcile us to the world we live in."

A clue to Dickens's gift of portraiture is to be found in his confession that he used to console himself for his small troubles when a boy by impersonating his favourite characters in the novels he read.

"I have been Tom Jones[7] (a child's Tom Jones, a harmless creature) for a week together. I have sustained my own idea of Roderick Random for a month at a stretch. . . . I have seen Tom Pipes go climbing up the church steeple; I have watched Strap with a knapsack on his back, stopping to rest himself upon the wicket-gate and I know that Commodore Trunnion held that club with Mr. Pickle in the parlour of our little village alehouse."

Dickens's approach to character was that of the actor, not that of the philosopher or the psychologist. The actor who is a fine artist. He observed from the outside, he built up character boldly and swiftly, catching the salient features, and his cut-and-thrust method triumphed because it resulted in something unforgettably vivid. Life was always surprising him and forcing him to keep in a state of constant excitement about it. Dickens did not need the co-operation of the reader, he only wanted his delighted approval. Nothing is suggested; everything is clearly presented. It is as if Dickens caught life grimacing and clicked the shutter—the result is both ludicrous and lifelike.

Genius he had in plenty, but it was untutored, and the restless fertility in contriving situations and inventing characters was never pruned by concern for form. Dickens added little to the development of the novel; it remained in his hands what it had been in the eighteenth century, a picaresque tale with a moral bias or the happy blending of drama and narration. Perhaps the author was less intrusive than formerly and the marshalling of climaxes undertaken at more breathless speed, but Dickens discloses no conscious artistic purpose—he is quite indifferent to the medium he uses.

Apart from his supreme value as an entertainer in fiction Dickens earned the gratitude of posterity for awakening the social conscience. In an age marred by callousness and complacency Dickens never lost faith in fundamental human goodness. Although he could see with clear eyes the stronger impersonal evil created by society, he continued to believe in the kindly fatherhood of God and in the triumphant power of love. Organization, whether political, charitable or religious, he rejected; the law killed, and spirit and systems, no matter how efficient, were no substitutes for

---

7. Tom Jones is a character in Henry Fielding's novel of the same name; the other characters in the excerpt come from the novels of Smollett.

the warm human relationships that were based on man's responsibility for his fellows. In his ideal of spontaneous
benevolence flowing from some inexhaustible fountain of
human goodness Dickens saw the great solvent of the grief
and misery that poisoned life around him.

Dickens is the Victorian age in fiction, or a large part of it.
He shared its faults of taste, its love of melodrama, its exu-
berant vitality, its belief in the sharp division of humanity
into sheep and goats. He shared, too, the innate optimism of
the period. His novels, humour apart, are morality plays in
which the good angels win the battle for the soul of man,
which is just what the majority of the Victorians were sure
they would.

George Eliot: The Imaginative Philosopher

John Holloway

John Holloway argues that George Eliot is a sage—a consistently serious writer whose works resemble classical drama or epic poetry. Holloway supports his view by identifying special features of Eliot's novels: their philosophical as well as ethical messages, imaginative stories that convey abstract principles, and the portrayal of the complex interconnectedness experienced by an ordinary family or community edging slowly through historical changes. Holloway gives special attention to *Silas Marner*, which he says exemplifies these features. John Holloway taught English at Cambridge University in England and at the University of Athens. He is the author of *Language and Intelligence, The Charted Mirror, Story of the Night: Studies in Shakespeare's Tragedies*, and *The Colours of Clarity*.

George Eliot is quite plainly a novelist who is also a sage. She speaks in her letters of 'The high responsibilities of literature that undertakes to represent life'; she writes 'it is my way . . . to urge the human sanctities . . . through pity and terror, as well as admiration and delight', or 'My books have for their main bearing a conclusion . . . without which I could not have dared to write any representation of human life—namely, that . . . fellowship between man and man . . . is not dependent on conceptions of what is not man: and that the idea of God, so far as it has been a high spiritual influence, is the ideal of a goodness entirely human'. But there is really no need to turn to the letters. The didactic intention is perfectly clear from the novels alone.

In *Adam Bede*, for example—and it is George Eliot's first full-length work—she says that so far from inventing ideal characters, her 'strongest effort is . . . to give a faithful ac-

Excerpted from John Holloway, *The Victorian Sage: Studies in Argument* (London: Macmillan, 1953).

count of men and things as they have mirrored themselves in my mind'. Realistic pictures of obscure mediocrity serve a didactic purpose: 'these fellow-mortals, every one, must be accepted as they are . . . these people . . . it is needful you should tolerate, pity and love: it is these more or less ugly, stupid, inconsistent people whose movements of goodness you should be able to admire'. Finally, she gives the lesson an autobiographical import: 'The way in which I have come to the conclusion that human nature is lovable—. . . its deep pathos, its sublime mysteries—has been by living a great deal among people more or less commonplace and vulgar'.

But George Eliot is not interested only in people and in their good and bad qualities; she wishes, beyond this, to impart a vision of the world that reveals its whole design and value. Her teaching may be partly ethical, but it is ethics presented as a system and grounded on a wider metaphysical doctrine. Her early novels emphasize how an integrated scheme of values is a help to man—'No man can begin to mould himself on a faith or an idea without rising to a higher order of experience'—and she vividly indicates the forces in her own time that impelled men to seek such a scheme. For one class to be cultured and sophisticated another must be 'in unfragrant deafening factories, cramping itself in mines, sweating at furnaces . . . or else, spread over sheepwalks, and scattered in lonely houses and huts . . . where the rainy days look dreary. This wide national life is based entirely on . . . the emphasis of want. . . . Under such circumstances there are many . . . *who have absolutely needed an emphatic belief:* life in this unpleasurable shape demanding some *solution* even to unspeculative minds . . . something that good society calls "enthusiasm", something that will present motives in an entire absence of high prizes . . . that includes resignation for ourselves and active love for what is not ourselves.' This is an interesting passage for the social historian, and for the critic of nineteenth-century capitalism too; but its present importance lies in showing what was of concern to George Eliot as she wrote, and how we are justified in searching her novels for philosophy as well as ethics.

ELIOT'S PARTICULAR STORIES BEST CONVEY HER BROADER MESSAGE

Moreover, she clearly saw that these principles did not lend themselves to abstract presentation; to be convincing they needed the methods of the imaginative writer. A striking passage in *Janet's Repentance* asserts that the influence which really promotes us to a higher order of experience is 'not calculable by algebra, not deducible by logic, but mysterious . . . ideas are often poor ghosts . . . they pass athwart us in thin vapour, and cannot make themselves felt. But sometimes they are made flesh; they . . . speak to us in appealing tones; they are *clothed in a living human soul, with all its conflicts, its faith.* . . . Then their presence is a power . . . and we are drawn after them with gentle compulsion.' We cannot but recognize, even in passing, how Dinah Morris, Maggie, Dorothea and others of George Eliot's characters are just such incarnations. And when, in *The Mill on The Floss,* she writes of the influence of Thomas à Kempis,[1] this appeal of a nonlogical kind is related directly to how books are written. The *Imitation* still 'works miracles' because 'written down by a hand that waited for the heart's prompting'; expensive sermons and treatises that lack this essential carry no 'message', no 'key' to 'happiness' in the form of a key to understanding; their abstractions consequently cannot persuade.

Thus it is clear that George Eliot wished to convey the kind of message, and knew that she must use the distinctive methods, with which this enquiry is concerned. But in examining how her novels are moulded to conform to these requirements, there is something which is here of first importance as it was not with [Benjamin] Disraeli. For George Eliot was a profoundly, perhaps excessively serious writer, and her novels are coloured through and through by her view of the world, and devoted in their whole dimensions to giving it a sustained expression, whereas most of Disraeli's novels are of lighter weight, and give expression to his more serious views more or less fitfully. It would, with George Eliot, be therefore a mistake to begin by noticing incidents, metaphors, snatches of conversation, or similar details. What must be given primary stress is the broad outline, the whole movement of her novels as examples of life that claim to be typical. 'How unspeakably superior', wrote Matthew Arnold, 'is the effect of the one moral impression left by a great action treated as a whole, to the effect produced by the most striking single thought or by the happiest image.' This

---

1. a German monk who wrote Christian mythical works, including the *Imitation of Christ*

is as true of the work of the sage-novelist as it is of classical drama or the epic poem. To ignore it is to miss the wood for the trees.

Silas Marner Exemplifies Eliot's Method

Silas Marner, perhaps because it is simple and short, shows this most plainly. It is worth examining in some detail. Silas the weaver, expelled from his little nonconformist community through a trick of blind chance, settles as a lonely bachelor in the obscure Midland village of Raveloe; one son of the local landlord steals his savings but is unsuspected, and Eppie, the daughter of another by a secret marriage, appears as a foundling at his cottage and he adopts her. Many years after, when she is a young woman about to marry, and her father Godfrey is middle-aged and has married again, the truth about her birth and about the robbery comes at last to light. Various things lend the tale its distinctive quality. First, the characters and their doings seem to belong to the same order of things as the non-human world that surrounds them. The little village, off the beaten track in its wooded hollow, is half submerged in the world of nature. The villagers are 'pressed close by primitive wants'. The passage of time and the rotation of the seasons affect humans and animals and plants all alike. Individuals are dominated by their environment. 'Marner's face and figure shrank and bent themselves into a constant mechanical relation to the objects of his life, so that he produced the same sort of impression as a handle or a crooked tube, which has no meaning standing apart.' It follows from this that all the people in the book are humble and obscure; they may be attractive or virtuous, but they are all nobodies. Silas is a poor weaver who finds hard words in the prayerbook, Godfrey Cass is a squireen's son and a barmaid's husband, Eppie marries a gardener—even Nancy Lammeter, Godfrey's second wife, is only a trim farmer's daughter who does the baking and says ''oss'. Such, the tale implies, is the staple of men and women.

The pattern of events in which these people are involved is one of 'poetic justice': vice suffers, virtue is rewarded. Silas, though unfortunate at first, is a good man, and at last is made happy. Godfrey Cass, who refused to acknowledge his daughter, has no children by his second marriage. Dunstan Cass the rake, stealing Silas's money at night, falls into the pond and is drowned. But this justice is rough and partial. It is not vindictively stern, so much as impersonal and aloof and half-known; it takes a slow chance course, and meets human imperfections not with definite vengeance but with a drab pervasive sense of partial failure or limited success. For the peasantry of such places as Raveloe 'pain and mishap present a far wider range of possibilities than gladness and enjoyment'. For Silas in his time of misfortune the world is a strange and hopeless riddle. His money is taken, Eppie arrives, through the operation of forces that he venerates without comprehending. Done injustice by a sudden twist of fate, he comes to trust in the world again over a long period of years, as the imperceptible influence of Eppie gradually revives long-dead memories and emotions; over the same period his estrangement from the other villagers is slowly replaced by intimacy. His life is governed by habit, and so is theirs. We never learn whether his innocence ever became clear to the congregation that expelled him as a thief.

Though the book is so short, its unit of measurement is the generation: Silas young and old, Eppie the child and the bride, Godfrey the gay youth and the saddened, childless husband. The affairs of one generation are not finally settled except in the next, when Silas's happiness is completed by Eppie's marriage, and Godfrey's early transgressions punished by her refusal to become Miss Cass. Dunstan Cass's misdeeds are not even discovered until, twenty years after the robbery, his skeleton is found clutching the money-bags when the pond is drained; and this is brought to light through, of all things, Godfrey's activities as a virtuous, improving landlord. Well may the parish-clerk say 'there's windings i' things as they may carry you to the fur end o' the prayer-book afore you get back to 'em'. All in all, the world of the novel is one which, in its author's own words, 'never *can* be thoroughly joyous'. The unhappiness in it comes when natural generous feelings are atrophied by selfishness: Dunstan steals, Godfrey denies his daughter. And the consequences of sin are never quite obliterated; Godfrey must resign himself to childlessness, though resignation is itself a kind of content. Real happiness comes when numb unfeeling hardness, the state of mind for example of the grief-stricken and disillusioned Silas, slowly thaws to warmer emotions of kindliness and love.

This novel contains, therefore, though in little, a comprehensive vision of human life and the human situation. It does so through its deep and sustained sense of the influence of environment and of continuity between man and the rest of nature, through its selection as characters of ordinary people living drab and unremarkable lives, and through the whole course of its action, working out by imperceptible shifts or unpredictable swings of chance to a solution where virtue is tardily and modestly rewarded, and vice obscurely punished by some dull privation. The details of George Eliot's treatment operate within this broader framework.

ELIOT'S NOVELS SHOW HISTORICAL CHANGE

Most of George Eliot's other books express the same vision of life, some of them amplifying it through their greater length or complexity. All except *Romola* and *Daniel Deronda* are set in the same historical period—that of the immediate past. This choice is significant. It is a time sufficiently near the present for manners to be familiar, dull and unremarkable, and for nothing to have the excitement or glamour of the remoter past; and yet sufficiently remote for the rhythm of life to be slower, and for man to be more fully subservient to nature. . . .

Adam Bede (1859) opens in the year 1799, when the village carpenter sings hymns as he works in his shop, and travellers go a-horseback, and 'there was yet a lingering after-glow' from the time of Wesley.[2] The actions of *Middlemarch* (1871–2) and *The Mill on the Floss* (1860) seem also to be set in the 1830s; while *Silas Marner* (1861) is a story of the early nineteenth century 'when the spinning wheels hummed busily in the farmhouses' and pallid weavers, 'like the remnants of a disinherited race', were to be seen 'far away among the lanes, or deep in the bosom of the hills' and 'to the peasants of old times, the world outside their own direct experience was a region of vagueness and mystery'.

The total impact of the novels also owes much to the sense they create of historical change; and of how, slowly, indirectly, in unexpected ways, it touches the lives of the characters. Inconspicuous as it is, this does much to suggest an integrated social continuity, of which personal relations between characters are only one part. *Janet's Repentance* portrays the gradual permeation of rural life by Evangelicalism;[3] it records one instance of a general social change. The back-

2. Charles Wesley wrote thousands of hymns; his brother John founded the religion Methodism.   3. relating to the group in the Church of England that stresses personal conversion and salvation by faith

ground of *The Mill on the Floss* is the expanding prosperity and material progress of the whole nation; and when the fortunes of the Tulliver family are at their lowest, Tom is carried up again by the rising prosperity of the firm he works for, with its many interrelated and developing commercial activities. At one point the story hangs upon whether or not to install a steam plant in the Tulliver's old watermill. When *Silas Marner* goes back at last to the chapel in Lantern Yard where he worshipped as a young man, he finds everything swept away to make room for a modern factory with its crowds of workpeople. In *Felix Holt*, personal experience is determined by the Reform Bill's gradually taking effect, and still more by the slow shift of population from agriculture to industry.

ELIOT'S NOVELS PROJECT COMPLEX INTERCONNECTIONS IN ORDINARY LIVES

But in this respect there is a more massive contribution. Real historical change is quite important in these novels, but it is less important than the complex interaction of town and countryside, of the pleasures or amusements of life with its work and business, of the various classes of society, and of social institutions like the church, the village inn, the bank, the chapel, the manor, the school and the workshop. It is an interesting contrast with [Charles] Dickens. Varied though his social panorama may be, he is really interested in the occupations of only one social class—his business men are rarely seen in their offices, and if they are, it is usually not to work—and an occupation interests him not for its distinctive niche in the scheme of things, but for what it has of odd or picturesque or *macabre*. His characters sell curiosities or optical instruments or skeletons; they drive coaches or keep inns; they are ham actors, dancing-masters, fishermen; or if simply clerks or schoolmasters, they tend to be oddities or rogues in themselves. But for George Eliot every character has his distinctive occupational niche, and it is this which determines his nature and gives him what leverage he has upon the course of the action. Lawyer Dempster in *Janet's Repentance*, Mr. Tulliver in *The Mill on the Floss*, Lawyer Jermyn in *Felix Holt*, Bulstrode and Mr. Vincy and Caleb Garth and Lydgate in *Middlemarch*, Tito in *Romola* even— all of them have their livelihoods to earn, and their actions are largely governed by the need to do so in a world that is complex and slow to change.

Often these complexities are not treated fully in the novel, but they lend it a depth and variety of social colour. Adam Bede's getting a wife and following a career are not two processes, but one; and as the story proceeds, the relation between him and Arthur Donnithorne is a product of how they stand as rival lovers, and how they stand as landlord and bailiff. In *Middlemarch*, the love-affair of Lydgate and Rosamond is largely a projection of their social and economic standing. . . .

Seeing the characters thus enmeshed in a wider context develops in George Eliot's readers the sense of a tortuous, half-unpredictable, slowly changing world of a thousand humdrum matters. 'Anyone watching keenly the stealthy convergence of human lots, sees a slow preparation of effects from one life on another . . . old provincial society had its share of this subtle movement; had not only its striking downfalls . . . but also those less marked vicissitudes which are constantly shifting the boundaries of social intercourse, and begetting new consciousness of interdependence . . . municipal town and rural parish gradually made fresh threads of connection—gradually, as the old stocking gave way to the savings-bank, and the worship of the solar guinea became extinct . . . settlers, too, came from distant counties, some with an alarming novelty of skill, others with an offensive advantage in cunning.' Lydgate exemplifies the first of these types, Bulstrode the second. The author, illustrating the general order of life by particular cases, is at pains to ensure that we see the wider drift.

ELIOT'S LESSONS PLAY OUT OVER TIME

George Eliot also uses the temporal scale of her novels for didactic ends. The slow movement of the natural world is stressed by the great span of time with which every novel deals—a span not packed with events in their variety, but necessary if we are to watch the full working out of even one event. *Silas Marner, The Mill on the Floss* and *Amos Barton* (if we take count of its epilogue) actually narrate events over a full generation. All of the other novels or *Scenes*, except *Adam Bede*, plunge back a full generation to depict the circumstances that originally created the situation of the novel. In *Felix Holt*, for example, the fortunes of all the chief characters except Felix are settled by the liaison, thirty-five years ago, between the local landowner's wife and her lawyer, and by the elderly minister's marriage as a young man to a Frenchwoman whose infant daughter is now a grown woman. *Daniel Deronda* tells how Daniel recovered the Judaic heritage of which he was deprived at birth. It is the same with the others.

The sense of a deterministic world where everything happens of necessity is increased in these novels by their stress on kinship. George Eliot is never tired of emphasizing how the nature of the parents fixes that of their children. *Felix Holt* depends for its climax on a visible resemblance between father and son. The earlier pages of *The Mill on the Floss* are full of the power of family tradition, the manner in which children reproduce and yet modify their parents' characters, and above all, the sense that kinship by blood is the basis of just such a slowly operating, half-inarticulate interdependence between things as George Eliot desires us to recognize everywhere. The reader who responds to this will see an added point when Maggie rescues Tom from the flood. The details of the narrative may leave much to be desired. But Maggie's action shows how a deep sentiment of kinship may overcome years of hostility; and in essence, it is apt in the same way as Aunt Glegg's sudden change to helpfulness when her niece is in trouble. It is not pure melodrama or pure sentimentalism at all. Again, in *Adam Bede,* the author is careful to bring out the partial resemblance and partial contrast between Adam and his mother, or Mr. Irwine and old Mrs. Irwine, or Mrs. Poyser and her niece Dinah the Puritan. There is a sustained sense of continuity by blood decisive in its influence but almost too obscure and subtle for observation. If there were any doubt that this contributes to a general impression of nature, the point is made explicitly in *Daniel Deronda.* When Daniel tells Mordecai, his Jewish future brother-in-law, that he too is a Jew, Mordecai's first words indicate how this kinship adumbrates a wider system: 'we know not all the pathways . . . all things are bound together in that Omnipresence which is the plan and habitation of the world, and events are as a glass wherethrough our eyes see some of the pathways'. Kinship is an aspect of the system of Nature.

Victorian Literature Reconsidered

Modern Attitudes Toward Victorian Fiction

Lionel Stevenson

Lionel Stevenson traces the history of critical attitudes toward Victorian fiction, which was ignored or deplored through the first half of the twentieth century. Stevenson cites renewed attention from modernist critics, new publications of biographical material about Victorian writers, and the discoveries of psychoanalysts and cultural anthropologists as causes for new attention to and respect for Victorian fiction. Lionel Stevenson taught English at the University of Southern California and at Arizona State College. He is the author of *Appraisals of Canadian Literature* and *Darwin Among the Poets*.

[Since World War II] critical and scholarly opinion has undergone a radical transformation in its attitude toward the works of the mid-nineteenth-century novelists. Prior to [World War II], the whole literature of the Victorian period languished in the depths of critical disfavor, and the novels were considered if possible even more contemptible than any of the other literary genres. When I was a graduate student I would scarcely have ventured to confess that I had read the works of [Charles] Dickens, [William Makepeace] Thackeray, and the Brontës, let alone that I enjoyed them.

The principal reason for this neglect, of course, was the normal cycle of literary taste which inevitably revolts against the immediately preceding era, and only the more violently when that preceding era has been especially eminent and revered. As long as the Victorian age was reviled for smugness, sentimentality, and vulgar taste, the fiction that reproduced it so faithfully was bound to incur those strictures to the extremest degree.

A particular reason for the antipathy toward the novel was

Reprinted from Lionel Stevenson, "The Modern Values of Victorian Fiction," *CLA Journal*, September 1960, by permission of the College Language Association.

the rigid code of critical dogmas that began to come into effect after 1880. [Critic and novelist] Henry James confidently proclaimed that the art of the novel depended essentially upon exact realism, with the corollary that the author's personal views and feelings ought to remain invisible. George Moore reinforced James's influence by propagating the French naturalistic school's doctrine that fiction must depict human behavior—mainly its violent and bestial manifestations—with the ruthless impartiality of an anatomist's dissection.

Not only by practical example in their own novels but also by persuasion in their prefaces and critical essays, James and Moore established the primacy of realism so effectively that the English fiction of the preceding generation appeared hopelessly naïve and archaic. The authoritative treatises that were published in the 1920's, notably *The Craft of the Novel*, by Percy Lubbock, and *Aspects of the Novel*, by E. M. Forster, were written by devout Jamesians who could not conceive that his axioms could ever be challenged.

Being blissfully unaware of these austere axioms, the Victorian novelists had given emotional coloring to everything they wrote about; they had expressed their own attitudes and sympathies without constraint; they had written in individual styles that sometimes burst into the extravagance of oratory or the luxuriance of poetry; their complicated plots had often included melodramatic suspense or farcical absurdity; many of them were committed to overt social purpose, and yet paradoxically their earnest crusades were so mingled with genial laughter that literal-minded students could accuse them of irresponsibility.

The critics and scholars in the early twentieth century could not be oblivious to the fact that a great many people still enjoyed reading the fiction of the earlier era; but this became merely another count in the indictment. Anything that existed primarily to give pleasure to a wide indiscriminate audience was automatically debarred from the sacred canon of good literature.

EARLY MODERNISTS ACKNOWLEDGED VICTORIAN AUTHORS

A general revival of appreciation for Victorian literature was certain to occur as soon as the era faded far enough into the past to make possible a normal perspective. The artistic and intellectual stature of the Victorian authors, and their astonishing variety of achievement, began to be tentatively and grudgingly acknowledged by pontiffs of modern criticism such as [poet] T.S. Eliot and [American critic] Edmund Wilson. As the tensions of this present age of anxiety increased, readers turned nostalgically to the literary landscape of an epoch that seemed to enjoy security and confidence. As soon as intelligent people started to read Victorian literature without preconceived notions, they discovered with amazement that the major authors, far from being the complacent optimists depicted in the accepted stereotype, were vitally concerned with the basic issues of social change and were distressed by most of the current trends of their century. A new explanation for the temporary eclipse of the great Victorians became apparent: the reading public of the early twentieth century had ignored them in an instinctive evasion of the disquieting warnings that the average person was unwilling to accept or even to perceive. The Victorians had been all too prescient in their anxiety about such a materialistic and competitive society as the modern world proceeded to adopt.

The Victorian novel naturally shared in the restored prestige of its period. The mid–nineteenth century was the first epoch when prose fiction had reached full parity with the other types of literature in critical esteem, and had surpassed them in popular appeal. Hence the combined opportunities of fame, profit, and influence attracted a wide assortment of ambitious and able authors, who might otherwise have expressed themselves in the older literary media. The energy and richness of Victorian fiction more than compensates for occasional deficiencies in technical skill. In fact, one of the most compelling reasons for studying Victorian fiction is that it offers a unique opportunity for observing a new literary genre in the very process of maturing. Each author was supplying his individual component, all were experimenting freely and borrowing from one another, while no rigid system of critical theory had yet come into existence to dictate practice and to prohibit innovation. By analysis of Victorian fiction we can learn a great deal about the processes of literary evolution.

RECENT SCHOLARLY RESEARCH
FOCUSES ON VICTORIAN FICTION

To account for the abrupt accession of interest in the Victorian novelists, cynics may suggest that the pressure upon professors to find new material for publishable books and articles, and upon graduate students to select topics for dissertations, obliged them to venture beyond the approved areas of scholarly research, and that Victorian fiction by its very bulk proved to be a virtually inexhaustible territory for exploration. It is true that adequate interpretation and explication had been impossible without certain indispensable tools of a sort that can never be satisfactorily provided until a couple of generations have elapsed. The most noteworthy of these tools are Gordon Ray's massive edition of Thackeray's letters, Gordon Haight's of George Eliot's, Bradford Booth's of [Anthony] Trollope's, Edgar Johnson's exhaustive biography of Dickens and Ray's of Thackeray, all of which have appeared [since 1950]. Indeed, the solid three-volume Nonesuch collection of Dickens's letters, which was hailed as a scholarly landmark when it was published in 1938, is already so obsolete and undependable that a vast new edition, three or four times as extensive, [was in the late 1960s] in preparation.

Once provided with the essential sources of factual information, the analysers were able to work more confidently upon the novels. When [critic] Bradford Booth in 1945 cautiously started a journal to facilitate communication among the scattered scholars who shared his interest in Anthony Trollope, he was amazed by an inundation of articles on other Victorian novelists also; he changed the name of his periodical to *Nineteenth-Century Fiction,* and it is now firmly established among the important academic quarterlies.

The resurgence of Victorian fiction, however, cannot be attributed primarily to the quest for a new area of research, or to the provision of documents and biographical data and the establishment of new media of publication, or even to the general rehabilitation of all Victorian writers. A more definite reason can be found in the influence exerted upon critical theory by the psychological study of the unconscious.

The dominance of realism in the novels of the late nineteenth century was postulated upon the rationalistic assumptions of the physical scientists. Henry James concerned himself exclusively with the conscious processes in the minds of his characters; and in his determination to avoid overt discussion of them he was obliged to show the characters engaged in interminable analytical discussion of their own and one another's motives and attitudes. Even the naturalists, who claimed to be displaying the primitive instincts of their characters rather than the intelligent decisions, nevertheless accepted the scientific method of tracing a logical train of cause and effect in human conduct. The novelists of the early twentieth century, such as [H.G.] Wells and [John] Galsworthy, who enlarged their focus to include the study of social groups and movements, were just as fully committed to scientific principles.

The Influence of Psychoanalysts and Cultural Anthropologists

All this cool reasonableness was invalidated when the theories of [Sigmund] Freud and [Alfred] Adler and [Carl] Jung gained currency. The psychoanalysts concentrated upon the irrational element in behavior; and since prose fiction is the literary form best suited to detailed recording of what goes on within individuals, the novelists promptly undertook to find ways of revealing the inner processes that are not susceptible to coherent exposition.

To communicate the impression of dreams and reveries and all the divagations of each individual's reactions to experience, it became apparent that the novelist must use distortions, metaphors, rhythm, incongruity, and any other possible stimuli to emotional and imaginative response that they could devise. Moreover, the psycho-analysts soon joined hands with the cultural anthropologists to emphasize the primitive and traditional elements in our mental equipment. Myths, folklore, and fairy tales gained new significance. The theories of Miss Maude Bodkin and Miss Jessie Weston about archetypes and symbolic ritual exerted immense influence upon critics and creative writers alike. In the second decade of the twentieth century the most enterprising writers of fiction were seeking for methods of combining these age-old intuitions and legends with the sophisticated externals of modern civilization.

The experimental fiction of [the 1920s] seemed to be radically new because it broke away from the tedious uniformity of external realism. Ironically, however, scholars are now realizing that [D.H.] Lawrence and [James] Joyce were at the same time paving the way for a restored appreciation of the Victorian novelists. Foreshadowings of the "stream of consciousness" have been recognized in early novels of Dickens, particularly in his studies of fear and guilt in such criminals as Bill Sikes [in *Oliver Twist*] and Jonas Chuzzlewit [in *Martin Chuzzlewit*]. Another recent critic has pointed out an affinity between Molly Bloom's drowsy reverie at the end of [James Joyce's] *Ulysses* and Flora Finching's scatter-brained conversation in [Charles Dickens's] *Little Dorrit.*

Once the shibboleths of external realism were abandoned, Dickens could no longer be dismissed as a mere caricaturist because he exaggerated and distorted the appearance and behavior of his characters, or as a mere sensationalist because he portrayed emotional agonies. Emily Brontë [author of *Wuthering Heights*] ceased to be regarded as a neurotic girl who spun an implausible horror-story out of her reading of [poet Lord] Byron. George Meredith [author of *The Ordeal of Richard Feverel*] was relieved of the stigma of wilful obscurity and gratuitously oblique implications.

COMMON ELEMENTS IN POETRY AND FICTION

One result of the changed critical attitude has been a weakening of the artificial barrier between prose fiction and poetry. Simile and metaphor, rhythm and echo, fantasy and symbol are now accepted as serving valid functions in a novel as well as in a poem. And this in turn has led to a more exact study of the art of fiction. The old assumption used to be that the Victorian novelists were "natural story-tellers" who simply rambled on through interminable sequence of confused episodes. Now students are discovering structural design, verbal patterns, recurrent images, symbolic correspondences, and all manner of other technical subtleties that were previously invisible mainly because a novel is so much larger and more complex than a poem that its minute aesthetic details are less conspicuous.

In the long run, the chief value of the revulsion in critical and scholarly opinion is that intelligent people can now undertake the reading of Victorian fiction without a guilty conscience. Exempted from the tyranny of categorical condemnation, we can approach each novel with an open mind, ready to appreciate its particular merits and leniently to observe its incidental defects. One must remember, of course, that the relationship between author and reader was vastly different a hundred years ago. It would be unwise to pick up [Thackeray's] *Vanity Fair* or [Dickens's] *Bleak House* or [Trollope's] *Framley Parsonage* or [George Eliot's] *Middlemarch* like a paper-back murder-mystery at an airport newsstand, to while away the three hours of a jet flight. Most of the Victorian novels came out serially in weekly or monthly installments, often running for as long as two years; and ordinarily they were read aloud in the family circle, a few pages every evening, to prolong the enjoyment to the utmost. One of the most pleasurable features of Victorian fiction is the refuge that it provides from the precipitate tempo of the modern age. The ideal procedure in reading a novel by Thackeray or Dickens, [Charles] Kingsley or Mrs. [Elizabeth] Gaskell, [George] Borrow or [Edward] Bulwer-Lytton is to forget about technical analysis and stylistic devices, to spread the reading over several weeks as an intermittent relief from more strenuous tasks, and to enter with imaginative sympathy the author's fully realized world, which is just as vivid as the actual world around us, just as unreasonable in its mixture of triviality and crisis, of absurdity and profundity, just as frustrating in its unreconciled tensions, and which nevertheless in some elusive way is an individual work of art, surviving apart from temporal vicissitudes. After one has finished reading such a novel for the sheer pleasure of the vicarious experience that it provides, one can then look back over its voluminous bulk and recognize the artistic dexterity and the creative insight with which it was constructed.

CHRONOLOGY

1830

William IV ascends throne; Charles Lyell, *Principles of Geology;* workers riot; Alfred, Lord Tennyson, *Poems, Chiefly Lyrical*

1832

First Reform Bill; Tennyson, *Poems*

1836

Charles Dickens, *Pickwick Papers*

1837

William IV dies; Victoria ascends throne; Thomas Carlyle, *The French Revolution;* Dickens, *Oliver Twist*

1838

People's Charter published, demanding voting rights and representation in Parliament; first locomotive enters London; Dickens, *Nicholas Nickleby*

1840

Marriage of Queen Victoria and Prince Albert; annexation of New Zealand; Penny Postage Act; Dickens, *The Old Curiosity Shop, Barnaby Rudge*

1841

Carlyle, *Heroes, Hero-Worship, and the Heroic in History*

1842

Mine Act, barring young children from work in underground mines; anesthesia first used in surgery; Chartists riot; railway from Manchester to London opens; Tennyson, *Poems (contained new poems and revised versions of some work from the 1832 volume);* Robert Browning, *Dramatic Lyrics*

1843

First telegraph line; William Wordsworth named poet laureate; Carlyle, *Past and Present;* John Ruskin, *Modern Painters,* volume 1; Thomas Babington Macaulay, *Critical and Historical Essays;* Dickens, *A Christmas Carol, Martin Chuzzlewit*

1845

Irish potato famine; Robert Browning, *Dramatic Romances and Lyrics;* Carlyle, *Oliver Cromwell*

1846

Dickens, *Dombey and Son;* William Makepeace Thackeray, *Snobs of England;* the Brontë sisters, *Poems by Currer, Ellis, and Acton Bell*

1847

British Museum opens; Charlotte Brontë, *Jane Eyre;* Emily Brontë, *Wuthering Heights;* Thackeray, *Vanity Fair*

1849

Charlotte Brontë, *Shirley;* Dickens, *David Copperfield;* Macaulay, *History of England,* volumes 1 and 2; Ruskin, *Seven Lamps of Architecture*

1850

Wordsworth dies; Tennyson named poet laureate; Dickens founds *Household Words;* Tennyson, *In Memoriam;* Elizabeth Barrett Browning, *Sonnets from the Portuguese*

1851

Great Exhibition at Crystal Palace

1852

Matthew Arnold, *Empedocles on Etna, and other Poems;* Dickens, *Bleak House;* cardinal John Henry Newman, *The Idea of a University*

1853

Arnold, *Poems;* Thackeray, *English Humorists of the 18th Century*

1854

Founding of Working Men's College, London; Crimean War begins; construction of London Underground begins; Dickens, *Hard Times*

1855

Arnold, *Poems, II;* Robert Browning, *Men and Women;* Dickens, *Little Dorrit;* Tennyson, *Maud and Other Poems*

1857

Ruskin, *Political Economy of Art;* Thackeray, *The Virginians*

1859

Charles Darwin, *Origin of Species;* Dickens, *A Tale of Two Cities;* George Eliot, *Adam Bede;* Tennyson, *Idylls of the King*

1860

Thackeray founds *Cornhill* magazine; Dickens, *Great Expectations;* Eliot, *The Mill on the Floss*

1861

Prince Albert dies; Elizabeth Barrett Browning dies; Arnold, *On Translating Homer;* Eliot, *Silas Marner*

1864

Public Schools Commission; Robert Browning, *Dramatus Personae;* Dickens, *Our Mutual Friend;* Newman, *Apologia pro Vita Sua*

1865

Arnold, *Essays in Criticism, I;* Lewis Carroll, *Alice's Adventures in Wonderland*

1867

Second Reform Bill; Arnold, *New Poems;* Carlyle, *Shooting Niagara—and After*

1869

Imprisonment for debt abolished; Arnold, *Culture and Anarchy*

1870

Forster's Education Act, making elementary education available to all children; Dickens dies; Dante Gabriel Rosetti, *Poems*

1871

Abolition of religious test at universities; trade unions legalized; Carroll, *Through the Looking-Glass;* Eliot, *Middlemarch;* Darwin, *The Descent of Man*

1873

Arnold, *Literature and Dogma*

1874

Thomas Hardy, *Far from the Madding Crowd*

1875

Public Health Act; Trade Union Act; Arnold, *God and the Bible*

1878

Electric lights installed on some London streets; economic

depression; Hardy, *The Return of the Native*

1879

First telephone exchange opens in London; Robert Browning, *Dramatic Idyls, I*

1880

Compulsory education; Robert Browning, *Dramatic Idyls, II*; Tennyson, *Ballads and Other Poems*

1881

Married Women's Property Act; Carlyle, *Reminiscences*; Robert Louis Stevenson, *Treasure Island*

1884

Third Reform Bill

1886

Hardy, *The Mayor of Casterbridge*; Stevenson, *Dr. Jekyll and Mr. Hyde, Kidnapped*

1887

Queen Victoria's Golden Jubilee

1888

Arnold, *Essays in Criticism, II*; Arnold dies

1891

Free Education Act; Hardy, *Tess of the D'Urbervilles*; Rudyard Kipling, *The Light That Failed*

1892

Tennyson dies

1894

Stevenson dies; Hardy, *Jude the Obscure*; Kipling, *The Jungle Book*

1895

H.G. Wells, *The Time Machine*

1897

Victoria's Diamond Jubilee; Kipling, *Captains Courageous*; Wells, *Invisible Man*

1898

Hardy, *Wessex Poems*; Wells, *The War of the Worlds*

1901

Queen Victoria dies; accession of Edward VII; Kipling, *Kim*

FOR FURTHER RESEARCH

ABOUT QUEEN VICTORIA AND VICTORIAN ENGLAND

E.F. Benson, *Queen Victoria.* London: Longmans, Green, 1935.

Hector Bolitho, *The Reign of Queen Victoria.* New York: Macmillan, 1948.

John W. Deery, *A Short History of Nineteenth-Century England.* London: Blandford Press, 1963.

Joan Evans, ed., *The Victorians.* Cambridge, England: The University Press, 1966.

Daniel Pool, *What Jane Austen Ate and Charles Dickens Knew: From Fox Hunting to Whist—The Facts of Daily Life in Nineteenth-Century England.* New York: Simon and Schuster, 1993.

Philip A.M. Taylor, ed., *The Industrial Revolution in Britain: Triumph or Disaster?* Lexington, MA: D.C. Heath, 1970.

ABOUT VICTORIAN LITERATURE IN GENERAL

Françoise Basch, *Relative Creatures: Victorian Women in Society and the Novel.* New York: Schocken Books, 1974.

Edith C. Batho and Bonamy Dobrée. *The Victorians and After.* London: Cresset, 1938.

David Cecil, *Victorian Novelists: Essays in Revaluation.* Chicago: University of Chicago Press, 1958.

G.K. Chesterton, *The Victorian Age in Literature.* Notre Dame, IN: University of Notre Dame Press, 1913.

John D. Cooke and Lionel Stevenson, *English Literature of the Victorian Period.* New York: Appleton-Century-Crofts, 1949.

Daniel G. Hoffman and Samuel Hynes, *English Literary Criticism: Romantic and Victorian.* New York: Appleton-Century-Crofts, 1963.

Robert Morss Lovett and Helen Sard Hughes, *The History of the Novel in England.* Boston: Houghton Mifflin, 1932.

Jo McMurtry, *Victorian Life and Victorian Fiction: A Companion for the American Reader.* Hamden, CT: Archon Books, 1984.

Alice Meynell, *Hearts of Controversy.* New York: Charles Scribner's Sons, n.d.

Barry V. Qualls, *The Secular Pilgrims of Victorian Fiction: The Novel as Book of Life.* Cambridge, England: Cambridge University Press, 1982.

Herbert L. Sussman, *Victorians and the Machine: The Literary Response to Technology.* Cambridge, MA: Harvard University Press, 1968.

Basil Willey, *Nineteenth Century Studies: Coleridge to Matthew Arnold.* New York: Columbia University Press, 1949.

Austin Wright, ed., *Victorian Literature: Modern Essays in Criticism.* New York: Oxford University Press, 1961.

ABOUT INDIVIDUAL VICTORIAN WRITERS

Bernard Bergonzi, ed., *H.G. Wells: A Collection of Essays.* Englewood Cliffs, NJ: Prentice-Hall, 1976.

Margaret Howard Blom, *Charlotte Brontë.* Boston: Twayne, 1977.

Harold Bloom and Adrienne Munich, eds., *Robert Browning: A Collection of Critical Essays.* Englewood Cliffs, NJ: Prentice-Hall, 1979.

Elizabeth Deeds Ermarth, *George Eliot.* Boston: Twayne, 1985.

Ina Ferris, *William Makepeace Thackeray.* Boston: Twayne, 1983.

George H. Ford and Lauriat Lane Jr., eds., *The Dickens Critics.* Ithaca, NY: Cornell University Press, 1961.

Elizabeth A. Frances, ed., *Tennyson: A Collection of Critical Essays.* Englewood Cliffs, NJ: Prentice-Hall, 1980.

Albert J. Guerard, ed., *Hardy: A Collection of Critical Essays.* Englewood Cliffs, NJ: Prentice-Hall, 1963.

Hugh Martin, *The Faith of Robert Browning.* Richmond, VA: John Knox, 1963.

J. Hallis Miller, *Charles Dickens: The World of His Novels.* Cambridge, MA: Harvard University Press, 1958.

Robert Brainard Pearsall, *Robert Browning.* New York: Twayne, 1974.

Virginia L. Radley, *Elizabeth Barrett Browning.* New York: Twayne, 1972.

Irving S. Saposnic, *Robert Louis Stevenson.* Boston: Twayne, 1974.

J.M.S. Tompkins, *The Art of Rudyard Kipling.* Lincoln: University of Nebraska Press, 1959.

Thomas A. Vogler, ed., *Twentieth Century Interpretations of Wuthering Heights: A Collection of Essays.* Englewood Cliffs, NJ: Prentice-Hall, 1968.

WORKS CONSULTED

Richard D. Altick, *Victorian People and Ideas*. New York: W.W. Norton, 1973.

Jerome Hamilton Buckley, *The Victorian Temper: A Study in Literary Culture*. Cambridge, MA: Harvard University Press, 1951.

John D. Cooke and Lionel Stevenson, *English Literature of the Victorian Period*. New York: Appleton-Century-Crofts, 1949.

Margaret Drabble, *For Queen and Country*. New York: The Seabury Press, 1978.

Bernard D. Grebanier et al., eds., *English Literature and Its Backgrounds*. Vol. 2, *From the Forerunners of Romanticism to the Present*. Rev. ed. New York: Dryden, 1949.

Robert Morss Lovett and Helen Sard Hughes, *The History of the Novel in England*. Boston: Houghton Mifflin, 1932.

Hazelton Spencer et al., eds., *British Literature: 1800 to the Present*. Vol. 2, 3rd ed. Lexington, MA: D.C. Heath, 1974.

Herbert L. Sussman, *Victorians and the Machine: The Literary Response to Technology*. Cambridge, MA: Harvard University Press, 1968.

George Tillotson, *A View of Victorian Literature*. Oxford: Clarendon Press, 1978.

T. Walter Wallbank and Alastair M. Taylor, *Civilization Past and Present: From the Beginnings of the Modern Era to the Present Time*. Vol. 2. Chicago: Scott, Foresman, 1949.

Michael Wheeler, *English Fiction of the Victorian Period, 1830–1890*. 2nd ed. New York: Longman, 1994.

Anthony Wood, *Nineteenth Century Britain: 1815–1914*. New York: David McKay, 1960.

INDEX